NEVILLE CHAMBERLAIN

Cover illustration 'Neville Chamberlain', lithograph by Andrew MacLaren, 1940. National Portrait Gallery, London.

Acknowledgments

The publishers would like to thank the following for their kind permission to reproduce copyright illustrations in this volume

Punch Publications, p. 41, p. 46, p. 94; *The Tribune*, p. 71; David Low, Evening Standard/Centre for the Study of Cartoon and Caricature, University of Kent at Canterbury, p. 90, p. 92; Zollkofer AG, p. 103.

To the memory of F. S. Northedge and K. R. Stadler.

A.NO = 010527
C.NO = 942·084

British Library Cataloguing in Publication Data
Neville, Peter
   Neville Chamberlain: A Study in Failure?. –
   (Personalities & Power Series)
   I. Title II. Series
   941.084092
   ISBN 0-340-56308-7

First published 1992

Typeset by Litho Link Ltd, Welshpool, Powys, Wales.
Printed in Great Britain for the educational publishing division of Hodder and Stoughton Ltd, Mill Road, Dunton Green, Sevenoaks, Kent by St Edmundsbury Press, Bury St Edmunds.

CONTENTS

NEVILLE CHAMBERLAIN –
A MALIGNED PRIME MINISTER?

Neville Chamberlain has had one of the worst presses of any modern Prime Minister. For his enemy, David Lloyd George, he was a 'pin-head' who would have made a good Lord Mayor in a lean year, while the great historian A.J.P. Taylor described him as 'efficient, conscientious and unimaginative'. Roy Jenkins, the biographer of Chamberlain's longstanding colleague Stanley Baldwin, has also written that it was as well that Baldwin, and not Chamberlain, was Prime Minister at the time of the 1936 Abdication Crisis because he would 'have alienated the country by treating the King like a negligent Town Clerk of Birmingham'.

Historians have generally paid insufficient attention to the formative influences in Neville Chamberlain's earlier years. Greatest of these was his father Joseph Chamberlain, 'Radical Joe', Birmingham's most famous politician, and an influential Colonial Secretary at the time of the Boer War. Neville's issues in his political career were often to be Joe's issues of tariff reform and urban improvement; throughout his life, the son was in awe of the father's achievements. He never, for example, thought that he could match his father's oratory and for many years remained a diffident public speaker. He also lived in the shadow of his half-brother Austen who was Chancellor of the Exchequer at forty. Indeed, he showed no particular interest in politics until his thirties.

Neville Chamberlain was a late starter. He was forty before he married Anne de Vere Cole (who warmed a somewhat frosty exterior) and nearly fifty before he became an MP. Thereafter be rose rapidly to the top, but early setbacks were not forgotten.

One was the Bahamas experience, when Neville spent six hard years trying to grow sisal on the islands of Andros (see pp 11-12) but failed. Any young man was likely to be marked by such a failure which cost his father £50,000.

Then there was his disastrous experience as Director of National Service in the First World War (see pp 18-20). This made him a lifelong enemy in Lloyd George, and created deep doubts about his fitness for a career in national politics. But by then, Chamberlain had been Lord Major of Birmingham, made a good job of it, and acquired the resilience to survive hard knocks.

Another enduring theme of Neville Chamberlain's life was his love of Birmingham. His father was nicknamed 'Brummagem Joe' and the city treated him almost as a mediaeval prince. It was a hard act to follow, but Neville succeeded in doing so both as councillor, alderman, Lord Mayor and MP. He gave the city an orchestra, and was a keen supporter of its university and its hospitals. Until his forties he was a Birmingham businessman who had the respect of his workforce, and provided the rest of his family with most of its income.

His family was close knit. Until his seventies Neville wrote regularly to his sisters Hilda and Ida, and also corresponded with his half-brother Austen when both were busy public men. He was devoted to his wife Annie. 'I'd never have done it without Annie,' he used to say.

With his father, he was respectful, if slightly awestruck but as Neville grew older, contemporaries noticed how he, rather than Austen, grew to resemble the older man. Joe himself regarded Neville as the cleverer of the two but told friends that Austen was the politician in the family. A historian has written that Joseph Chamberlain's 'characteristic sally was the sneer delivered with a poker face, broken by a distinct curl of the lip'. Political opponents of both father and son might have recognised the description. Neville Chamberlain was frequently accused of being cold, arrogant and sarcastic. But this is not the image that emerges from his personal correspondence with his sisters, friends and political colleagues. It seems reasonable to suggest that a rather blighted, hard youth gave Chamberlain a tough protective shell to protect an innate reserve and lack of confidence, which he tried too hard to compensate for.

THE REFORMER

Neville Chamberlain's achievement as a domestic reformer seems considerable. He phased out the Poor Law in 1929 and put the economy back on a sound footing after the economic disaster of 1929-31. As Health Minister in the 1920s, he was responsible for massive schemes of house-building and slum clearance (see pp 46-7).

Yet recognition of the achievement has often seemed niggardly. Chamberlain's budgets in the 1930s were attached by A.J.P. Taylor as 'truly reactionary' because they 'reversed the trend towards direct taxation which had been going on for nearly a century'. Again, although Chamberlain's first, and perhaps best, biographer, Keith Feiling, wrote of how he used the tariff protection policy inherited from his father 'to recover prosperity', Taylor cast doubts on the genuineness of the conviction. Thus Chamberlain, in introducing his Import Duties Bill in February 1932, made 'pious references to the memory of his father' and over the whole issue of protection 'no one displayed emotion except Neville Chamberlain; even his display was unconvincing'. That was not the reaction of those who were there. The response to Chamberlain's speech in the Commons was tumultuous (see pp 23-4). It is as if the disdain of anti-appeasors has also to be directed at Chamberlain's genuine achievement as a social reformer, although, curiously, A.J.P. Taylor was to attack Chamberlain not for appeasing, but for not carrying appeasement far enough.

THE APPEASER

One of the great myths about Chamberlain has been that he was a narrow-minded parochial businessman, with no comprehension of foreign affairs. In fact, he was interested in foreign affairs even before he entered public life (see p 24). He was also widely travelled in Europe, North America and Asia. These facts are easily available, yet they seem to count little against his fateful statement about Czechoslovakia being 'a faraway country of which we know nothing' in 1938.

Although Chamberlain's appeasement policy sprang from his loathing of war, an abiding hatred, he was never a pacifist. Before the First World War he had lobbied in Birmingham for more defence spending and he retained an interest in that sphere when he entered government. Neither was he pro-

German. Indeed, he is on the record as saying that he found Germans 'extremely stupid' and on another occasion as Chancellor of the Exchequer, bemoaning the fact that he had been forced to lease a house to the odious German ambassador Joachim von Ribbentrop. Years earlier, after a visit to the Black Forest, Chamberlain had exclaimed, 'How I loathe the Germans'. Whatever, therefore, the appeasement policy of the 1930s was based on, as operated by Chamberlain, it was not love of Germany! Joe Chamberlain, by contrast, had been an admirer of Germany and campaigned for an Anglo-German alliance in the 1890s.

The key to Chamberlain's foreign policy lay in his hatred of war, but also in his desire to spend the state's resources on schools, hospitals and roads. In this sense, appeasement was for Chamberlain the extension of the social reforms he had enthusiastically carried through in the 1920s. Experience as Chancellor of the Exchequer between 1931 and 1937 then gave him an acute appreciation of the finite nature of Britain's resources, and an understandable reluctance to spend them on tanks and guns.

Chamberlain is, of course, open to the criticism that he did not perceive the truly awful danger presented by Nazi Germany. Because he was used to reasoned debate with trade unionists, health committees and the like, it is said that he found dealing with gangster-like dictators difficult. But this was not due entirely to lack of experience, for as Chancellor he had dealt with foreign statesmen over issues like German reparations (pp 62-3). Rather it was perhaps that nothing in his background prepared him for dealing with Hitler. As he himself said in his broadcast to the British people after declaring war on Germany in September 1939, 'For it is evil things that we shall be fighting against: Brute Force, Bad Faith, Injustice, Oppression and Persecution'. These things were the antithesis of everything that Neville Chamberlain stood for.

But the stain left on Chamberlain's reputation by appeasement has been great, so great that his successor, Margaret Thatcher, felt obliged to apologise to the Czech president for the 'national shame' of Munich in 1990. It is perhaps an indication of the controversy that Chamberlain's foreign policy still arouses that Thatcher's successor John Major came to an opposite conclusion a year later. In acknowledging Chamberlain as one of his political heroes, and a great twentieth-century social reformer, Major remarked that 'I do not think he was as naive about Hitler as some people now claim'.

So great in fact has been the controversy about Chamberlain and appeasement been that both his domestic achievement and the real meaning of appeasement have totally obscured (see p 69). Ironically, it fell to Winston Churchill, the arch opponent of Chamberlain's policy in the 1930s, to give one of the best analyses of what Chamberlain had been trying to do. 'Those who are prone,' Churchill wrote,

> by temperament and character to seek sharp and clear cut solutions of difficult and obscure problems, who are ready to fight whenever some challenge comes from a foreign power, have not always been right. On the other hand, those whose inclination is to bow their heads to seek patiently and faithfully for peaceful compromise are not always wrong.

Chamberlain's policy was to seek 'peaceful compromise' with Germany; in doing so, however, he jeopardised the security of the Czech state.

The stereotype of the 'Umbrella Man' of Munich, therefore, died hard, but Chamberlain concluded that no alternative policy was available. The evaluation of his entire career has tended to hinge on the assessment of this judgement.

2

JOE'S BOY

Arthur Neville Chamberlain, to be known throughout his life as Neville, was born on 18 March 1869 to Joseph and Florence Chamberlain. It was Joseph's second marriage, for his first wife Harriet had died six years earlier in giving birth to Neville's half-brother Austen. Florence was to be no more fortunate for having given Joseph another four children, she too died in childbirth in 1875. Young Neville had three sisters, Hilda, Ida and Ethel, and a half-sister in Beatrice, the other child of the first marriage.

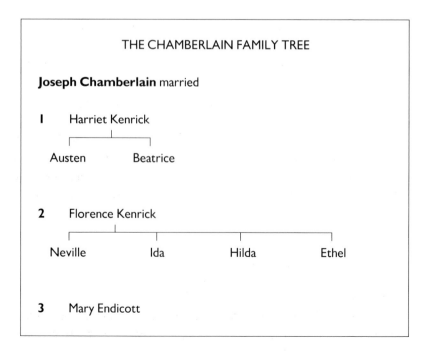

THE CHAMBERLAIN FAMILY TREE

Joseph Chamberlain married

I   Harriet Kenrick

Austen   Beatrice

2   Florence Kenrick

Neville   Ida   Hilda   Ethel

3   Mary Endicott

His childhood, therefore, could have been blighted by that curse of Victorian society, death in childbirth or its parallel, death in infancy. In fact, it was not.

The dominant figure in Neville's life was his father 'Brummagem Joe' who was, at the time of his birth, a rising local politician in Birmingham, and who in time, became one of the ablest political leaders never to be prime minister of his country. But Joe had been shattered by the loss of his first wife, and the death of Florence was another crushing blow. Years later he was to say of her,

> there is no thought or action of my later years which my wife has not shared with me, and no place or ambition or desire formed for the future which has not been shadowed by her death.

Six-year-old Neville had but the haziest memories of his mother, but one of his biographers writes that he 'was deeply conscious of her love'. He did have a vivid memory of his aunt telling him about his mother's death. The damage that could have been inflicted by this early trauma seems to have been offset by the warmth of his relationship with his sisters, especially Hilda and Ida, and the efforts of a series of aunts who came to run Joseph Chamberlain's household. He did not marry his third wife, the American Mary Endicott, until nearly thirteen years later, in 1888.

Neville seems to have inherited his mother's liveliness of spirit, but his father's looks and attention to detail. His relationship with Joe Chamberlain was formal, mingled with a degree of fear on the boy's part, while the preoccupations of politics and the loss of his two young wives made the father distant and withdrawn. Years later, Neville was to write of his father's 'piercing eye that few could face with comfort'.

This distance meant that it was Neville's godfathers who taught him to shoot and fish, hobbies which were to last a lifetime. Nevertheless, Joseph Chamberlain was never the brutal Victorian father figure (there is only one recorded instance of him striking his children, when Neville refused to get out of the bath!). But his children admired him from afar.

SCHOOLDAYS
—

In 1877, just before his eighth birthday, Neville Chamberlain suffered the fate that awaited most upper middle-class boys of that time and he was sent off to a boarding school, near Southport. He seems to have liked it well enough. In a letter to his aunt Clara, the boy wrote, 'I like the school though I miss you all very much'. But like many who went through a similar experience, young Neville resented the lack of privacy, 'there being six little beds' in his dormitory 'with only one screen and five little washingstands, beside which we have a bath every morning in the bathroom'. Cannily, the future Chancellor of the Exchequer told how he had only spent a little of his pocket money. 'I have spent sevenpence already, 'he wrote, 'but I do not mean to spend any more of it just yet.'

A second preparatory school proved to be an even less happy experience, and then Neville was sent to Rugby, famous as the school where Doctor Arnold of *Tom Brown's Schooldays* had presided as headmaster. For a boy like Neville Chamberlain, the son of a businessman, Rugby was more appropriate than Eton or Harrow, and Austen was already there is his last year.

Little is known of Neville's time at Rugby, and the little that is known shows that he detested the place (not the last British Prime Minister to have such a feeling about his old school!). He never went back to Rugby, except on the rare occasions when he had to change trains on the way to Birmingham.

Given that Neville disliked the emphasis on team games as Rugby, with its 'cold showers and cross country runs' ethos, this is hardly surprising. Matters were apparently made worse in the early stages by the fact that Neville was bullied by a boy whom Austen had beaten when he was a school prefect. Despite all Doctor Arnold's efforts, bullying was to be a distressing feature of public schools until well into the twentieth century.

Looking back later in his life, Neville remembered himself as a thin, rather nervous, adolescent who was painfully shy (he retained this characteristic into adult life). This tallies with a rare description from this time by a friend who recalled him as 'a slender, dark-haired boy, rather pale and shy who would sometimes talk quickly in a low voice about things that caught his sense of humour'. The reference to humour is striking, as it was not something political opponents remembered him for later.

Unsurprisingly, the adolescent Neville was rather put off politics by the obsessive talk about it in his father's house. He was apparently a most reluctant participant in a school political debate, and when a friend asked him why, Neville replied, 'You don't know what our house is like before my father makes one of his big speeches'. He then added rather waspishly, 'Wretched man, he never knows what he is going to say'. A surprising remark about a man then in Gladstone's government who was reckoned to be one of the finest platform speakers of his day, but one which, perhaps, reflected momentary adolescent resentment against a dominant father. Mealtimes at home could be tense, with Joseph Chamberlain preoccupied with business and political affairs.

Despite his dislike of Rugby, Neville did receive a more rounded education there than most of his fellow pupils. This was because Joe Chamberlain insisted, after Neville had mastered the traditional classics curriculum, that he be transferred to the so-called 'Modern Side'. This gave him an opportunity to study subjects like history and science, these being an innovation at Rugby. According to one of his biographers, H. Montgomery Hyde, this move may have boosted the shy boy's confidence for 'he found himself thrown in with a lot of smaller boys whose superior he felt himself to be'.

HIGHBURY

Neville's unhappiness at Rugby does not seem to have got him much sympathy at home. Joe Chamberlain was probably too busy to notice, and he also schooled his children to take life's hard knocks without complaining. Aunt Clara, while well meaning, ignored Neville's obvious misery on one occasion on his return from Rugby merely remarking, 'Neville, your cap's crocked!'

Nevertheless, as Neville grew up, the similarities between him and his father became more obvious, as the historian David Dilks has pointed out:

> In all these characteristics – grasp of the practical, distaste for organised religion, wide reading, fondness for good company, food and drink – Neville in later life bore a more than accidental resemblance to his father.

The point about religion is a significant one. The Chamberlains were Unitarians, and part of the Nonconformist community in Birmingham, but Joe lost his Christian faith to a large degree when Florence died. Neville, whilst tolerant of those who were sincere believers, disliked zealotry and preferred practical good works. But the Unitarian influence showed strongly in his belief in the virtues of hard work, and suspicion of those to whom success had come too easily.

A big change in Neville Chamberlain's life came in 1888 when Joe married Mary Endicott, the daughter of an American cabinet minister. Mary was actually younger than Beatrice and Austen, but got on extremely well with all six of the Chamberlain children. She also helped Joe to mellow in old age as he himself admitted and 'brought my children closer to me'. Even Queen Victoria, who had been shocked by the political language of 'Radical Joe's' early career, apparently approved of the marriage!

It was for Mary that Joe built Highbury, a spacious house in the Birmingham suburbs (where Neville was still living as a company director in his thirties). It was the centre of a lively social life, where Joe Chamberlain was visited by the greatest in the land, and the scene of the lively debates covering every aspect of the arts and sciences which were a feature of the Chamberlain family. Here, Neville came to share Joe's love or orchids (he always wore one in his buttonhole, leading to ghastly puns in *Punch* about Orchid [awkward] questions) and many hours were happily whiled away on Sunday mornings inspecting the glasshouses where they were grown. With characteristic thoroughness, Neville who made a catalogue of his father's orchid collection.

Eventually, after Joe's death in 1914, Highbury was bought by Birmingham Corporation from Austen who had inherited it. As its name suggests, the house was named after the part of North London where Joe Chamberlain's family had lived before he came to Birmingham in 1854.

BAHAMAS AND BUSINESS

After leaving Rugby, Neville Chamberlain attended Mason College (later part of the University of Birmingham) where he studied metallurgy and engineering. The question of Neville attending university, as Austen had done, never seems to have arisen. His father had earmarked a business career for him, and had him apprenticed to a local firm of accountants. Neville did well and his employers wanted to keep him on, but his father's dominant influence decided otherwise.

The Bahamas Connection

In 1890, Joe Chamberlain took his young bride on a visit to her native United States, and they also visited Canada as well. In Montreal, they met the Governor of the British Bahamas islands, who persuaded Joe that much money could be made from growing sisal on the islands. According to the

Governor, one Ambrose Shea, the plant grew 'like a weed' on the islands, and could be used to make the finest hemp, an essential product for ropemaking.

Joe was readily converted, not least because he had lost a lot of money investing in Argentine stock at home. He therefore cabled Neville to come out and take charge of the land he was prepared to buy in the Bahamas. The investment was a large one of fifty thousand pounds, about a million pounds in modern terms. The feelings of Neville, just twenty-one years old and embarking on a new career, about this can be imagined! He was being asked to uproot himself from his beloved Birmingham and move three thousand miles away into an alien culture and climate. Yet there is no evidence that Neville ever considered rejecting the proposal, so great was the authority of a Victorian father. Added to this was the genuine respect and admiration that all Joe Chamberlain's children had for him. For Neville, his trust in his father's judgment was to mean seven hard years as a sisal grower. But this judgment was, in this instance, to prove poor and the whole venture was a hazardous one as some of Joe's business associates vainly tried to point out. He was a hard man to shift once he had made up his mind.

The Bahamas Years

After the initial expedition to inspect sites on the islands, Neville returned to the Bahamas in 1891 and bought up a large tract of land on the island of Andros. He wrote to Joe saying that, 'I am confident that I have secured the best site in Bahamas'. On Andros he built a comfortable house, although like everyone else he suffered from the climate. Rubbish had to be burnt every evening to try and keep out the clouds of mosquitoes.

At first, the venture seemed to prosper. By the end of 1893, over four thousand sisal plants were being grown and this rose to six thousand by 1895, with Neville employing eight hundred labourers. He got on well with his black labourers (although odd remarks in letters home betray the prejudices of his class and race) who doted on their 'Mr. Chimblin'. Neville's birthdays were occasions for great celebrations with the islanders dancing (he noted) 'quadrilles and waltzes and gallops with a vigour that was most laudable on such a hot day'.

Plainly it was a lonely life; the only other Europeans were his overseer Knowles, his wife, and a Catholic priest. At times though, it could be an adventurous one. Neville had to kill tarantulas, and keep a four-foot snake in the storeroom to kill rats! He also developed his interest and skills in botany and entomology by studying island flowers and insect life.

By 1896, however, things began to look bleak. Mrs. Knowles died, and Knowles took to the bottle so much that he eventually had to be sent off the island. Worse, as Neville noted in a letter to his father, was the fact that 'the plants don't grow . . . I don't see how we can possibly last out longer than the end of March'. He felt the failure keenly and was unduly hard on himself, writing that 'In spite of all that you and Austen said before, this is my failure. I can't bear to think of it'.

In reality, it was Joe's failure as much as Neville's. But to admit such a failure, at the age of twenty-seven, when his half-brother was already an MP and a rising political star, was galling. As it was, his father was understanding, but the fifty thousand pounds had to be written off. In some senses, it was Neville, rather than Joe, who lost most from the Bahamas experience. His youth was effectively gone, and with it went the opportunity to have a social life which would have been there in Birmingham. There was momentary bitterness in a reference to Andros as 'that awful hole'. Soon though, Neville was able to look back on the Bahamas years as 'a great experience'. He was too busy to be bitter for long.

What significance did the Bahamas period have on Neville's life? He had matured as a person, and learnt to be self-reliant in a way not open for most young men of his class and background. Certain character traits were further emphasised, like his passion for self-improvement (he read widely while on Andros), while others were developed which are reminiscent of his father. One was a sense of public duty and responsibility, so that the most distressing aspect of the sisal-growing failure for Neville was the fact that 'all my people will relapse into what they were is extremely distressing to me'. He was to show equal concern for his employees in Birmingham.

A MAN OF BUSINESS

After the Andros fiasco, Neville Chamberlain embarked on the business career which his father had originally earmarked for him. His uncle Arthur originally obtained an opening for him with an armaments firm, but Joe Chamberlain thought that this might be politically embarrassing for a government minister like himself. So Neville obtained a directorship with the firm of Elliotts in Birmingham which made copper, brass and yellow metal. There, he was able to indulge his interest in social improvement by introducing a surgery on the premises for workers, welfare supervisors, and benefits for injured men and their dependents. Eventually, he became chairman of the board at Elliotts.

Neville's major business interest, however, was in the small firm of Hoskins & Son which specialised in making cabin berths for ships, and was later to make hospital beds for the National Health Service. Writing to a friend in the Bahamas, Neville told of how he had 'bought another business which I am going to smash up all by myself', an obvious reference to the Andros experience so recently ended. Hoskins had only 200 employees, which made it easier for him to follow the paternalistic impulse he had inherited from his father. A pension scheme was soon introduced for the workforce along with a 5 per cent bonus for productivity, both indications that Neville Chamberlain was a go-ahead employer with a social conscience. He was proud of the fact that, his firm like that of his future political boss, Stanley Baldwin, never had a strike. Years later, a former worker at Hoskins was to write admiringly of his then employer: 'I do hope and pray I shall meet him in the next life.' The religious reference may read oddly to the modern reader, but its fervour underlines the point that Chamberlain did have the 'human touch'. Hoskins was the centrepiece of his life until 1914, and was also an important financial component in the welfare of the entire Chamberlain family.

Neville was never merely the dull Birmingham businessman of legend though, for his outside interests were many. He took a keen interest in local hospitals, sat on the management boards of several and took a special interest in Birmingham General. He was also on the governing body of Birmingham University, following on the work of his father, who was the University's first Chancellor. Somehow, too, he found time to be a Sunday School teacher, as well as Secretary of the city's Liberal Unionist Association.

POLITICS

The last-named appointment was significant. Although Neville had lost that loathing of politics that he had felt as a schoolboy, he didn't want a life in politics for himself. His father had left the Liberal Party in 1886 over the issue of Irish Home Rule, and his small group of so-called Liberal Unionists had subsequently allied themselves to the Conservatives. This brought office in the Conservative administration of 1895 to 1906 to Joe as well as to Austen (at one point Joe was Colonial Secretary and Austen Postmaster-General).

Neville supported both of them enthusiastically, especially over the issue of preference for imperial goods (imperial preference), which caused Joe to leave the Conservative government in 1903. As a businessman in Birmingham he had first-hand experience of the threat to local industry from cheap foreign manufactured goods, and like his father and brother, he also believed that goods from the British Empire should receive preference over those from other countries. This belief, together with filial loyalty, caused Neville to campaign for his father in the elections of 1900 and 1906 while at the same time 'speaking as often as my nervousness and laziness permit me (which is not much)'. This was self-deprecation, and while no one could ever accuse him of laziness, Neville Chamberlain was still acutely shy in public and found speaking an ordeal when faced with a large audience. He had watched his father bewitch audiences on many occasions, and felt quite overawed.

It was a difficult inheritance, doubly so since Austen became Chancellor of the Exchequer in 1903 when barely forty. It seemed that Neville, although described by his father as 'the clever one', would keep out of politics unless it involved trying to get family members elected. If he had any desire for the high affairs of state in which his brother was involved, there was no evidence of it in the immediate years that followed his return from the Bahamas.

JOE'S DEATH

Once convinced of the need for tariff protection and imperial preference, Joe Chamberlain decided to resign from Balfour's cabinet, and wage a great campaign against Free Trade, a sacred cow in British politics since the repeal of the Corn Laws in 1846. The Conservative Prime Minister, A.J. Balfour, was a reluctant convert to protectionism because of the fear of 'stomach taxes' which would inflate the price of basic commodities like bread. Neville Chamberlain remained enthusiatic about his father's cause and wrote that 'I am confident that we shall win. But whether we shall win at the next election is a much more doubtful affair'. This prediction proved to be only too accurate when the Liberals, completely united by the ancient cause of Free

Trade, routed the Conservatives and their Liberal Unionist allies in the 1906 general election. Only in Birmingham, by now Joe Chamberlain's private kingdom, did the cause of protection triumph, and in July 1906, Joe made what was to be his last great speech in the city. Urging yet again the need for imperial preference and tariff protection, Joe told his admiring audience that: 'The union of the Empire must be preceded and accompanied by a better understanding, by a closer sympathy.'

Two days later, Joseph Chamberlain suffered a severe stroke which paralysed his right side, and resulted in gradual loss of his sight and capacity for speech. He became, in the words of one historian, 'a pathetic invalid' and Neville lamented how his father, once a man of such vigour and independence, was now entirely dependent for his most basic needs on his wife Mary. Joe's only real pleasure now, wrote his youngest son, was in watching his grandchildren at play: 'He could not even talk to them. He could only make uncouth noises which often frightened them, and it was touching to watch his efforts to attract them.' He died on 2 July 1914, just a month before Britain entered the First World War, and was buried in Keyhill Cemetery in Birmingham with the other members of the Chamberlain family. (The family refused the offer of burial in Westminster Abbey to honour Joseph's last wishes.) Neville's immediate reaction was relief that eight years of intense suffering was at an end: 'I am glad to think his trials are over.' Family pride in Joe's achievements remained. Speaking of his father on the centenary of his birth in 1936, Neville said: 'The greatest service of Joseph Chamberlain to local government was the setting it on a new pedestal of dignity and honour.'

LORD MAYOR

Birmingham had provided Joseph Chamberlain with his first power base when he was Lord Mayor, and it also gave Neville the opportunity to cut his political teeth as well. Indeed Joe had lived to see Neville's first hesitant entry into the local political arena, when in September 1911 his son was adopted as Liberal Unionist candidate for the All Saints Ward in Joe's old constituency of West Birmingham. Two months later, Neville was elected to the council on a platform which stressed the need for town planning, open spaces, the desirability of better technical education and the extension of the canal system. He retained an interest in canals thoughout his life, although they were to prove something of a lost cause. Otherwise, the outline of Neville Chamberlain, the social reformer, with his concern for living and working conditions, was already there. Further promotion came in 1914 when Neville was elected an alderman, and in the following year, he was elected Lord Mayor of Birmingham.

MARRIAGE

As he entered his fortieth year, Neville Chamberlain had virtually reconciled himself to permanent bachelorhood. Earlier hopes of marriage to a professional singer had faded, and a busy life left little time for socialising. Then, to the amazement of all, Neville met Anne de Vere Cole, the attractive daughter of an army officer, and married her in 1911 after a whirlwind courtship. Annie, as Neville came to call her, was in her late 20s, and her husband's opposite in almost every way. Where Neville was punctual, Annie was always late, where he was punctilious about business affairs, she was disorganised, and while he was in close control of his emotions, Annie was warm and volatile.

Yet the match worked from the start despite Neville's disapproval of his new relatives and particularly his wild brother-in-law Horace. Amongst many extraordinary practical jokes, Horace's most bizarre trick was to disguise himself as Emperor of Ethiopia and arrive with a suitable entourage to inspect a Royal Navy Warship. To confuse the crew, Horace and his friends spoke a bewildering mixture of Latin and Greek before departing by train for London! When Annie told Neville about the latest jape of his twenty-eight year old brother-in-law, he remarked that Horace must 'be a little mad!'

Despite Annie's moods and occasional neuroticism, she proved to be a great asset in political campaigns, for she lacked her husband's inhibitions and would bicycle enthusiastically around his ward, and later his constituency, meeting people of all classes and backgrounds. Later, Neville was to recognise his debt to his wife, who remained tenaciously loyal to him. He was delighted when Annie gave birth to a daughter Dorothy in 1911, to be followed in 1913 by the birth of a son, Frank. And within his home, Chamberlain was able to unwind and devise exciting games for his two small children. Their memories make it clear that Neville was not a stuffy Edwardian father, and he was able to relate to his children far more naturally than Joseph Chamberlain had done. But he was nevertheless a private man, at ease only in his home, and his public persona made him seem unbending and sometimes harsh in judgement.

FROM TOWN HALL TO WHITEHALL

Neville Chamberlain proved to be a hard-working and patriotic Lord Mayor of Birmingham, anxious to do what he could for the war effort. But he also maintained his interest in improving the quality of life in the city, often in unusual ways. It was Chamberlain, for example, who, following the visit of the Manchester Hallé Orchestra to Birmingham in March 1916, proposed that the city should have its own 'first class orchestra' to be paid for out of the rates. The Birmingham Symphony Orchestra was founded in 1919 along with a large concert hall and cheap seats, making classical music available to the general public.

Another Chamberlain brainchild was the Municipal Savings Bank, set up after much pressure on the Treasury in London, which soon became a great success. Writing of his time as Lord Mayor in June 1916, Chamberlain noted how it was 'generally recognised that a new atmosphere of initiative and energy has been imported into the administration'. This recognition helped Neville to be re-elected for a second term as Lord Mayor in December 1916. His administrative prowess soon gained him a reputation outside the West Midlands.

In the meantime, events at the centre of power in London brought about changes which were to intimately affect Neville Chamberlain's future. In December 1916, the Liberal Prime Minister Asquith, long criticised for being an indifferent war leader, resigned and was replaced by the former Chancellor of the Exchequer, David Lloyd George. This change was very much at the demand of the Conservative and Unionist Party, now in the wartime coalition government, amongst whose leaders Austen Chamberlain was prominent. It was Austen who then drew the attention of Lloyd George to his brother's capacities.

Following a visit to London for a mundane conference on municipal borrowing, Neville Chamberlain was intercepted as he was about to get on his train home to Birmingham. He was told that Austen (then Secretary of State for India) wanted to see him at the India Office in the Strand. Austen then told him that Lloyd George wanted to see him at 10 Downing Street immediately.

At Downing Street, Lloyd George told Chamberlain that he was offering him the newly established post of Director-General of National Service. As Lloyd George wanted to announce the appointment to the House of Commons that same evening, Chamberlain had to make his mind up on the spot. Under pressure from his brother, and mindful of the national interest, Chamberlain felt obliged to accept.

He did so reluctantly. Later he confided to his diary that the new post was an appalling responsibility. It was also to prove something of a disaster.

CHAMBERLAIN AND LLOYD GEORGE

That evening Lloyd George told the House of Commons that: 'We have been fortunate in inducing the Lord Mayor of Birmingham to accept the position of Director-General under this scheme'. The scheme involved securing the *voluntary* recruitment of men and women for essential war work, so the reference to 'National Service' can confuse because, unlike the scheme operative after World War Two, it also applied to civilian and not to military service.

Neville Chamberlain ran into immediate difficulties because it was soon clear that Lloyd George didn't like him. According to Leo Amery, later a cabinet colleague of Chamberlain's and then Assistant Secretary to the War Cabinet, the basis for this dislike was an absurd physiological one, for Lloyd George fancied himself as something of a phrenologist who could judge men by the shape of their heads! 'When I saw that pin-head,' Lloyd George told Amery after his first meeting, 'I said to myself, "he won't be any use."' On such ridiculous personal prejudices can people's careers hinge.

In his own war memoir, Lloyd George wrote about the circumstances surrounding the appointment:

> He was appointed in a hurry, as I had to announce the appointment in the House of Commons in my speech on the policy of the new government. I had never seen him and I accepted his qualifications for the post on the recommendation of those who had heard of his business and municipal experience.

Setting aside Lloyd George's personal prejudice (which remained for a lifetime), the statement to the Commons hints at why the Chamberlain appointment was a catastrophic one. It was made far too hurriedly, without considering the vital issue of whether Chamberlain should be an MP or not.

The fact that he was not meant that other ministers, like the Minister of Labour, often hostile to the whole idea of National Service, had to defend Chamberlain in the Commons. Even at the most basic level Chamberlain had little or no idea of what his brief was, not knowing whether it extended to Scotland and Ireland, or even what his salary would be.

There were also errors on Chamberlain's side. He should have insisted on being given a seat in parliament, and the decision to appoint his former Town Clerk in Birmingham to be his chief aide in the Directorate may not have been a wise one because the man knew nothing of Whitehall practices. But throughout the brief period of seven months when he held the position of Director, Chamberlain was constantly obstructed by the War Ministry, the Ministry of Labour and the Unemployment Exchanges in his efforts to secure the transfer of industrial workers. So complete was the failure that by the time of Chamberlain's resignation just 3,000 volunteers for essential war work had been placed in employment.

Others recognised that this was not Chamberlain's fault. The Irish MP John Dillon remarked that 'if Mr. Chamberlain were an archangel, or if he were Hindenburg and Bismarck and all the great men of the world rolled into one, his task would be wholly beyond his powers', while his party leader Bonar Law believed that his commission was 'under the circumstances a hopeless task'.

The ill-feeling on Lloyd George's side was reciprocated in full. Chamberlain distrusted the Prime Minister's quicksilver brilliance and declined to receive any honours from him. Lloyd Geoge became notorious for selling off titles and honours, like the OBE, and Neville Chamberlain refused to be part of 'that rabble'.

After Chamberlain's departure, and under a new boss with a proper job description, the Department of National Service flourished. Chamberlain himself put his finger on the cause of his own failure later in a speech to his own Liberal Unionists in Birmingham. 'What was needed,' he said, 'was not a campaign for volunteers' but a 'careful and thorough survey of the whole resources of the nation in manpower and womanpower'. Nevertheless, Neville Chamberlain would have been less than human had he not been sorely disappointed by his experience as Director of National Service. Coming after the failure on Andros, it could have seriously undermined the self-confidence of a lesser man. He had hated 'the idea of resignation' but his family advised him to look for a parliamentary seat in Birmingham and he was soon adopted as Conservative and Unionist candidate for the Ladywood constituency. Despite this, he had been seared by the experience in London. His diary entry for 17 December 1917 read: 'My career is broken. How can a man of nearly 50, entering the House with this stigma upon him, hope to achieve anything.' An additional blow had been the death in the trenches of his cousin Norman, to whom Neville had been especially close. Norman, who was an officer in the Grenadier Guards, was machine-gunned with the rest of his company at the beginning of December, although it took some time for the news of his death to reach the rest of the family. Neville never forgot the circumstances of his cousin's death or the terrible war that brought it about, and he wrote with characteristic self-deprecation, 'His life was devoted to others and I feel a despicable thing beside him'.

Norman had written to Neville from the front telling him that the losses of trench warfare must never be allowed to happen again. Neville was always conscious of the fact that, owing to age, he had not fought in the war (of his contemporaries Baldwin did not, but Churchill did), and his foreign policy was later to be influenced by the memory of its horrors.

This bleak time in Chamberlain's life was not improved by an attack of gout (from which he suffered throughout his life) followed by both chicken pox and sciatica (in those days, there were special gout boots to ease the discomfort caused to the feet). But within a year, he had regained his health, his buoyancy, and won the seat for Ladywood in the so-called 'khaki election' of December 1918 immediately following the Armistice with Germany. This was despite the loss of his half-sister Beatrice who died in the great influenza epidemic of 1918-1919, which killed more people than the war itself.

Neville's Labour opponent was a Mr. Kneeshaw who had been a pacifist in the war, not fashionable sentiments in a campaign when one of the slogans was 'Hang the Kaiser'. His majority was a comfortable one of over 9,000, and he noted with delight how Annie, provided with a car which had been borrowed from Elliotts, threw herself into the campaign with almost manic enthusiasm. 'Middle-aged shopkeepers,' Neville wrote to his sister Ida were 'dragged forth from the recesses of their back rooms where they sit at tea' and made to take part in the Conservative campaign. But his own shyness in front of large meetings remained.

timeline	1869	Neville Chamberlain born
	1887	Leaves Rugby
	1890	Visits Bahamas
	1891	Begins period on Andros
	1896	Collapse of sisal growing scheme
	1903	Austen Chamberlain, Chancellor of the Exchequer
		Joseph Chamberlain begins tariff reform campaign
	1906	Joe Chamberlain dies
	1911	Neville marries Anne de Vere Cole
		Elected as councillor for All Saints Ward in Birmingham
	1915	Neville Chamberlain becomes Lord Mayor of Birmingham
	1916	Appointed Director of National Service
	1917	Resigns as Director of National Service
		Death of Norman Chamberlain in France
	1918	Neville Chamberlain elected MP for Birmingham Ladywood constituency

Points to consider

1) **In what ways was Neville Chamberlain affected by the fact that his father was a famous politician?**
2) **How significant an experience were the years in the Bahamas for Neville Chamberlain?**
3) **Explain why Chamberlain was a failure as Director of National Service in 1916-17.**

THE MAKING OF A POLITICIAN

It was his father's stroke in 1906 which began the process which propelled Neville Chamberlain into political life. Joe's condition, the seriousness of which was disguised from the people of Birmingham for many years, meant that increasingly Neville was asked to deputise for him at political meetings, despite his natural reticence.

TARIFF REFORM

A great cause united father and son. For as the historian David Dilks notes, Neville took to political life 'with a will and the fact tha the had long been a tariff reformer by conviction eased the transition'. By contrast, Austen was a tariff reformer by filial obligation rather than strong conviction.

Increasingly, therefore, in the years after 1906, Neville was welcomed at Liberal Unionist meetings in Birmingham to put the case for protection and imperial preference. He never forget his father's legacy and remembered it years later in 1932 when, in an economic climate which favoured tariff protection, it fell to him as Chancellor of the Exchequer to sound the death knell of free trade.

In a voice which another of his biographers notes began 'to falter with emotion' so that he had 'difficulty in controlling it as he conjured up his father's image', Chamberlain said:

> Nearly twenty years have passed since Joseph Chamberlain entered upon his great campaign in favour of Imperial Preference and Tariff Reform. More than 17 years have gone by since he died, without having seen the fulfilment of his aims and yet convinced

that, if not exactly in his way, yet in some modified form his vision would eventually take shape. His work was not in vain. Time and the misfortunes of the country have brought conviction to many who did not feel that they could agree with him then. I believe he would have found consolation for the bitterness of his disappointment if he could have foreseen that these proposals, which are the direct and legimate descendants of his own conception, would be laid before the House of Commons, which he loved, in the presence of one and by the lips of the other of the two immediate successors to his name and blood.

Members of the House of Commons cheered as Austen, then a backbencher, came down to the Government front bench to congratulate his brother.

Free trade was dead, and could never have survived the cold economic climate of the 1930s, but imperial preference proved to be a pipedream. Months after making this speech, Chamberlain represented Britain at the Empire and Commonwealth Conference in Ottawa but only obtained a declaration that the lowering or removal of tariff barriers would ease the movement of trade. Individual agreements between individual members of the Commonwealth would merely be 'a step forward which should in future lead to further progress in the same direction'. No such development ever took place, and Neville Chamberlain soon realised that his father's dream of imperial preference was no longer attainable.

IRISH HOME RULE

Joseph Chamberlain had left the Liberal Party in 1886 over the issue of Irish Home Rule, and Neville supported his father's position. This put him on the side of the die-hards in the Tory Party when the 1910 elections gave the Irish party the balance of power in the Commons and it demanded Home Rule. This was not to be his normal stance, but Ireland was after all the great cause of Liberal Unionism. Chamberlain himself was to take many years to describe himself as a 'Conservative' rather than a 'Unionist'.

When in office, however Chamberlain was to prove sympathetic in his handling of relations between Britain and the independent Irish Free State.

FOREIGN AFFAIRS

The stereotyped description of Neville Chamberlain has him as a middle-class businessman who had little knowledge of, or interest in, foreign affairs. This is inaccurate. He was well informed about defence matters, and made a significant contribution to the Navy League in Birmingham, while deploring the Liberal government's decision to reduce the strength of the army. This knocks on the head the attempt by some historians to portray Chamberlain as a pacifist (for example, Sidney Aster).

He also showed that scepticism about foreign alliances which was to be characteristic of him as both Chancellor of the Exchequer and Prime Minister. Britain had in 1904 agreed to an Entente Cordiale with France, and she followed this in 1907 with a similar agreement with Russia. Chamberlain voiced his reservations in a letter to a friend in 1908. 'The real enemy,' Chamberlain wrote:

> is Germany and they (the agreements) are even worse than useless against her. It seems to me that they may very possibly drag us into war but will be mighty little help if war should come. I do not mean by this that I disapprove of the understandings but I disapprove of the attitude of folding our arms and saying, 'Oh, it's all right no. Russia and France are squares so we can sleep easy'.

In another letter in the following year, Chamberlain (with a strong echo of what was to be his attitude in the 1930s) warned that the British had 'got to make ourselves too strong to be attacked'.

Far from being a pacifist during this period of his life, Chamberlain was outraged (as David Dilks emphasises), like all Unionists in Birmingham, when the Liberal government refused to lay down more than four Dreadnought battleships. The slogan of the day was 'We want eight and we won't wait,' and so great was the uproar that the Asquith government had to agree to launch a further four Dreadnoughts. Chamberlain declared that he had 'felt this horrible Navy crisis very deeply'.

HEALTH AND WELFARE

The interest in public health and welfare which was to be a feature of Chamberlain's political career, was also developed during his days as a Birmingham businessman. He had long been interested in the running of the city's hospitals, and with his usual practicality suggested a method of 'screening' patients in their out-patient departments. Instead of the chaotic situation caused by patients with trivial complaints being sent to the hospitals, this would allow some patients to be treated by their own doctors, and others to be assessed inside the hospital. Where necessary, a minor ailment could be dealt with by a nurse, while the most serious cases would be referred to a consultant. Common sense did previl in this instance, because although the Birmingham medical committee turned the scheme down, it was taken up later in London.

The sense of public duty which Neville had inherited from his father also meant in Dilks' words that he 'was incapable of assuming a duty unless he immersed himself in it'. Thus, the position of official hospital visitor, generally treated somewhat casually by other holders of that post, was taken completely seriously by Chamberlain. He was even known to go straight to hospital from Hoskins in his working clothes.

Another particular Chamberlain interest were the so-called Provident Dispensaries which provided health care for people at their place of work. He was also instrumental in persuading well-known surgeons and consultants to charge patients in the dispensaries only half their normal fee.

All this experience in the sphere of public health was to be invaluable to Chamberlain when he became Health Minister in the 1920s. By then, his Birmingham experience had given him a considerable degree of expertise in the field. As his biographer emphasises, the trouble which Neville Chamberlain went to in achieving mastery of the subject was a notable characteristic of his. He could never do things by halves. Chamberlain himself attributed his devotion to civic work partly to 'the tradition of the family and partly my own incapacity to look on and see other people mismanage things drive me to take up new and alas unremunerative occupations!'

If the last remarks can be seen as arrogant, this judgement needs to be balanced against the testimony of many who worked with him about Chamberlain's capacity as a negotiator, and his ability to cut through waffle to the essential point of a discussion.

The Greater Birmingham Bill

As the son of 'Brummagem Joe', Neville Chamberlain's first loyalty, after his family, was to the city of Birmingham. He, therefore, found himself intimately involved in the presentation to Parliament of the evidence needed to show that his native city needed to enlarge its boundaries threefold. Neville gave evidence in support of this revision of the city's boundaries to Committees in both the House of Commons and the House of Lords. The success of the campaign meant that Birmingham was now, in reality, what it had long claimed to be, 'the Second City of the Empire'. It also provided the final impetus for Neville Chamberlain's move into local politics in 1911.

THE TORY PARTY

Even before his entry into local politics in Birmingham, Neville Chamberlain was in touch with the highest circles of the Conservative Party. He was already on friendly terms with Leo Amery, a Birmingham MP and later a Cabinet colleague, who told him about the discontent with the then party leader, Arthur Balfour. By 1911, the campaign against Balfour had reached such a pitch that he was forced to resign, and Austen, as a former Chancellor of the Exchequer, looked well placed to succeed him. Neville certainly thought so and sent Austen a telegram summoning him back from holiday in Italy. But in the event, the Conservatives turned to the relatively unknown Bonar Law to be their leader, and Neville vented his disappointment in a letter to his brother telling him that he 'would have made the Party's fortune.'

All this, David Dilks points out, 'did nothing to sharpen Neville Chamberlain's appetite for national politics'. He felt that Austen, like his father, had been betrayed by his colleagues and denied the position of leader which was rightfully his. In Austen's case moreover, there was no reputation for youthful radicalism to live down, something which had always made the Tories suspicious of Joe Chamberlain.

YEARS OF APPRENTICESHIP

What then was the significance of the years between 1896 (when he returned from Andros) and Neville's entry into local politics in Birmingham in 1911? One obviously important development was that he lost that antipathy for politics that had been a feature of his youth although not entirely his nervousness about public speaking. Plainly his comment about 'laziness' was an absurdity, because his industry was incredible and it was more of a reflection on that self-deprecation which was typical of him. Neville Chamberlain was hard on himelf. Others were sometimes to feel that he was too hard on them.

The other point about those years of apprenticeship in Birmingham was that Neville showed that devotion to public affairs which had been such a strong characteristic of his father (although Neville had wider interests). The historian Lord Blake had divided modern prime ministers into 'actors' and 'doers,', and Chamberlain became a doer in Birmingham. There he developed that capacity for hard work and taking care over details which was to serve him well during his political career. He also became interested in issues like tariff reform, foreign affairs and public health, which were to become central concerns when he entered government.

4

CHAMBERLAIN IN GOVERNMENT

When Neville Camberlain was elected as MP for Birmingham Ladywood, his sister Hilda wrote to him saying, 'You are a natural leader of men'. The truth of this judgement was to be speedily demonstrated by Chamberlain's rapid rise in the Conservative and Unionist Party. But it was Austen Chamberlain who was the immediate beneficiary of the Lloyd George Coalition's victory in the 1918 general elections when the Prime Minister offered him his old post of Chancellor of the Exchequer.

Once a Member of Parliament, however, Neville became more conscious of the differences in political thinking between the two men. When they met after the election, Austen stressed the need for economy in the nation's finances, while Neville wanted more money for housebuilding in Birmingham and other schemes. While this may appear to merely reflect the fact that Austen was in the Government while Neville was not, Neville believed that their disagreement was more deepseated. 'He thinks me wild and I think him unprogressive and prejudiced,' he told Hilda, and of the two, Austen was perhaps the more natural Tory.

Wild or not, Neville soon made his mark in the House of Commons. In his maiden speech in March 1919 on the Rent Restriction Bill, Chamberlain spoke (without notes) in support of an amendment which prevented landlords imposing rent increases unless they could produce a certificate saying that their properties were fit to be lived in. This speech impressed the Attorney-General so much that he immediately inserted new wording into the Bill to cover the points Neville had made. And the *Birmingham Post* described Chamberlain's first parliamentary speech as 'an admirable performance'.

INTO OFFICE

—

Just a year later Neville was offered the junior position of Under Secretary to the Minister of Health. Yet this early recognition of his talents was tainted by the suspicion that it was a gesture from Lloyd Geoge to make up for the National Service disaster. Chamberlain turned it down, and his suspicions about Lloyd George were well justified. For when in 1920 some Irish Nationalist MPs put up his name to take over the post of Chief Secretary (Ireland was then moving to independence via the Government of Ireland Act), Lloyd George vetoed the appointment. 'I don't like that fellow,' he told a colleague, apparently tolerating the idea of 'that pinhead' in a minor government post, but not in a major one.

In the event, Neville Chamberlain did not have to wait long for advancement. In October 1922, the famous Carlton Club meeting for Conservative MPs decided to withdraw support for Lloyd George, thus forcing his resignation and the end of the wartime coalition. Austen stood loyally by Lloyd George and therefore lost office, the sort of characteristic action which prompted Lord Birkenhead's gibe that 'Austen always played the game, and always lost it'. But Neville had no such difficulty and shed no tears about the fall of his enemy. His dilemma was that when the new Prime Minister, Bonar Law, now heading a purely Conservative administration, offered him the post of Postmaster-General, Austen reacted, as Neville noted, 'very badly'. Creditably Neville offered to turn down the offer rather than harm his relationship with his half-brother, but Austen then urged him to accept. So after only three years in the House of Commons, Neville Chamberlain found himself in the Cabinet. His one regret was that Austen's loyalty to his old coalition colleagues kept him out of Bonar Law's government.

Promotion followed promotion as far as Neville Chamberlain was concerned, although his rapid rise was obviously assisted by the absence from government of Coalition Conservatives like his brother and Lord Birkenhead. Within months of accepting the position of Postmaster-General, he became Minister of Health and in this new post, he also attracted admiration. Bonar Law's deputy Stanley Baldwin noted early in 1923 how Chamberlain had done 'extraordinarily well in his new post'.

BALDWIN AS PRIME MINISTER

Baldwin's admiration was soon translated into further advancement for Chamberlain. This followed the retirement of Bonar Law on health grounds, and the elevation of Baldwin to the premiership. Chamberlain had initially supported the Foreign Secretary, Lord Curzon, for the post, but had not, he himself admitted, realised how unpopular Curzon was in the country. Curzon, that 'very superior person' as the popular rhyme had it, also suffered from the disadvantage of being in the House of Lords.

With Baldwin's appointment came about a partnership which was to dominate British politics for the next fourteen years. For one of Baldwin's first actions was to appoint Neville Chamberlain as his Chancellor of the Exchequer, when he realised that he could not hope to hold down both jobs himself (he began by doing so).

Chamberlain and Baldwin

Superficially the two men had a good deal in common. Both came from a business background (in Baldwin's case, the family firm of Baldwins Ltd., Ironmongers) and Baldwin's biographers described him as 'an excellent manager'. Like Neville Chamberlain, Baldwin had served his apprenticeship in local government both as a Justice of the Peace and a member of Worcestershire County Council for nine years. He, too, entered Parliament relatively late in life at forty, replacing his father Alfred as MP for Bewdley (by coincidence at the suggestion of Joseph Chamberlain) in 1908. Unlike Neville Chamberlain, however, it took Stanley Baldwin eight years to get a junior Government post.

Neville Chamberlain always had the greatest admiration for Baldwin's qualities, perhaps because, like Annie Chamberlain's, they were so very different from his own. Baldwin was, to use the modern phrase, 'laid back', slow in decision-making, prone to overlong contemplation, but generally sounder than Chamberlain in his appreciation of human beings and their moods and fancies.

Baldwin's personality has been well summed up by his biographer Roy Jenkins:

> He devoted a lot of time to the personal relationships of politics and to conducting them in a mollifying, unhurried way. This took priority over the reading of briefs, the annotation of Cabinet

papers, or the swift making of minor decisions. This was not a question of either niceness or laziness. It was a question of how he believed he could best attain his major political purposes.

Baldwin's belief in the importance of personal relationships was shown by the fact that he spent hours in the House of Commons chatting to fellow MPs of all parties, even when he was Prime Minister. By contrast, Chamberlain was never a 'House of Commons man' and was rarely to be found in the smoking room as Baldwin was. This characteristic of Baldwin's could be irritating. One colleague complained that there was little to be done with 'a leader who sits in the smoking room reading the Strand Magazine'. By contrast, Roy Jenkins notes that Chamberlain 'would never have read haphazardly'. Neither though did he develop the political antennae that Baldwin did, or have his ability to sense the mood of the House of Commons. In Robert Blake's classification, Baldwin is an 'actor' rather than a 'doer', and in Cabinet, his reluctance to make decisions or to steer discussions in any positive direction could be infuriating. Lord Curzon complained bitterly about his tendency to let discussions wander off 'into hopeless irrelevancies'. On another celebrated occasion during an important discussion about economics, Baldwin was seen to pass a note to Winston Churchill (then Chancellor of the Exchequer). It read: 'Matches. Lent at 10.30 am. Returned?'

For all that, Baldwin had great qualities of common sense and integrity, as Neville Chamberlain recognised. In 1923, he wrote admiringly of Baldwin's 'straightforwardness and sincerity', and the two men always remained friends. This esteem was reciprocated on Baldwin's part, and he persuaded Chamberlain to become Chancellor of the Exchequer when he himself doubted whether he had 'any gift for finance'.

In many respects, Chamberlain and Baldwin made an ideal combination, with the Prime Minister making up for his Chancellor's tendency to expect too much of others, and to ruffle their feelings. Writing years later, Chamberlain's private secretary at the Treasury recognised his mastery over the material, but expressed doubts over his man management.

> He was a pleasant chief though shy and reserved, so that those who worked for him could rarely discover the humanity and kindliness that were undoubtedly there.

This could lead to 'a certain fallibility in his judgement of persons and as a corollary to a lack of sureness in appraising political situations'. Baldwin, by contrast, might not have had Chamberlain's technical mastery of subjects but he had an instinctive understanding of his fellow Englishmen which Chamberlain lacked. Throughout the inter-war years, public opinion was mollified by the reassuring image of the nice, pipe-smoking Mr. Baldwin, that peeked out at the audience in contemporary newsreels or spoke in friendly tones on the radio. What it could not perceive was that behind the bluff and genial Stanley Baldwin was the workhorse Chamberlain, who was the powerhouse behind much Conservative legislation.

---

a note on . . .

THE POLITICS OF THE 1920s

The 1920s was a confusing decade with a tri-party system in which Labour was in the ascendant while the Liberals were in terminal decline. There were also two periods of minority government.

In 1923, the Conservatives remained the largest party in the House of Commons with 259 seats, but Labour (191 seats) formed a government under Ramsay MacDonald. This was because the Liberals (158 seats) were not prepared to support the Conservatives and kept Labour in office for 9 months.

In 1924, the Conservatives won a large majority over Labour and Liberals combined, but in 1929 there was a second Labour minority government. This time Labour were the largest party with 287 seats, but did not have an absolute majority over the Conservatives (261 seats) and the Liberals, now down to just 59 seats. However, the Liberals were prepared on this occasion to support the largest party in the House of Commons, whereas they had not been in 1923.

THE TARIFF ELECTION

In the event, Neville Chamberlain's first spell as Chancellor of the Exchequer was not to last long. It ended with the controversial decision by Baldwin to call an election in December 1923. The issue was tariff protection, the great cause of the Chamberlain family, and one which Neville backed to the hilt regardless of what some of his colleagues thought.

The question which has puzzled historians is why Stanley Baldwin called an election on such an issue, when he, like all Tories, could remember the 1906 disaster, when the issue of 'stomach taxes' had last been raised. Two factors seem to have been uppermost in Baldwin's mind. One was unemployment, which had been rising steadily since the war. Here the arguments of Leo Amery, the Colonial Secretary, were most effective, because Amery pointed out the folly of following a free trade policy when other powers were putting up tariffs to keep out British goods. This in turn caused lay-offs at home and pushed up unemployment. Baldwin, who also took advice from both the Chamberlain brothers, came to believe that some form of protection was needed if the unemployment figures were to be kept down.

The second factor is more contentious. Baldwin may have had evidence that Lloyd George, then away on a trip to the USA, was about to announce his support for protectionism and abandon free trade. Baldwin feared, it is alleged, that Lloyd George would then gang up with the old coalitionist Conservatives like Austen Chamberlain and Birkenhead (then out of office) and destroy the Tories by arguing for protection. Was this a likely explanation of Baldwin's decision? One historian believed that his decision was a result of his fear of Lloyd George, and the temptation to 'dish the Goat' (as Baldwin called Lloyd George – a reference to his womanising) by converting to protectionism before his arch enemy could (he despised Lloyd George even more than Chamberlain did). But this is not the view taken by Baldwin's biographers Keith Middlemass and John Barnes, who were altogether more cautious:

> There is no conclusive evidence to suggest that Baldwin decided on an immediate dissolution because of fear of what Lloyd George's return might bring; but there is no other plausible reason for his change of mind.

As it was, Baldwin's conversion was not complete. He was too nervous to impose so-called 'stomach' tariffs, but was prepared to do something for trade with the Empire. Chamberlain 'warmly welcomed' this conversion and told Hilda how the Prime Minister was

> disposed to go a long way in the direction of new duties with preference to help the Dominions and to develop Empire sugar,

cotton and tobacco, all of which we now have to buy from the USA.

Baldwin also proposed to give special protection to those areas of Britain suffering from unfair competition from abroad and to lobby for the reduction of foreign tariffs. All this mattered not a jot because Labour and the Liberals were able to raise the old cry about 'dear food'. The election of 1923, like that of 1906, was a disaster for the Tory party although it remained the largest party in the House of Commons with 257 seats. But Labour and Liberals combined could outvote the Tories, and Baldwin decided to let Labour as the second largest party, take office.

Throughout the campaign of 1923, Neville Chamberlain had been Baldwin's loyal lieutenant, and there is nothing to suggest that he, any more than the Prime Minister, foresaw the electoral disaster.

timeline		
	1918	Chamberlain elected MP for Birmingham Ladywood
	1919	(March) Chamberlain makes his maiden speech in the House of Commons
	1920	Chamberlain turns down Lloyd George's offer of the post of Under Secretary of Health
	1922	(October) Lloyd George Coalition falls after meeting of Conservative MPs at the Carlton Club. Neville Chamberlain made Postmaster-General
	1923	Chamberlain becomes Health Minister and then Chancellor. (December) Stanley Baldwin calls general election

Points to consider

1) **Outline the circumstances in which Neville Chamberlain rose to office between 1918 and 1922.**
2) **Assess the different qualities of Neville Chamberlain and Stanley Baldwin as politicians.**
3) **Why did Baldwin call an election in December 1923 and why did he lose it?**

5

HEALTH MINISTER

During the brief life of Ramsay MacDonald's first Labour Government, Chamberlain reverted once more to his first love and became Opposition spokesman on housing and health. In this position, he broadly supported the important Housing Act introduced by John Wheatley, Labour's first Housing Minister.

His most important achievement perhaps during this period was to persuade Baldwin to take the majority Tory coalitionists Austen Chamberlain and Birkenhead back into the leadership. The circumstances were characteristically Baldwinesque. Chamberlain had a chat with Baldwin in Saint James' Park and suggested a meeting between him and Austen over dinner (after Baldwin had shown a typical reluctance to address the point at their own meeting). This was to take place at Neville Chamberlain's house, and Baldwin was to boldly implement Neville's advice and offer Austen a place on the Conservative front bench, without his usual prevarication, which might offend Austen. To Neville Chamberlain's relief, Baldwin did just that and the two men were reconciled, all due, Neville noted a shade smugly in his diary, 'I may say to me'.

The Conservatives' swift return to office in October 1924 owed a good deal to the so-called 'Zinoviev Letter', allegedly from the head of the Communist Comintern and encouraging the outbreak of revolution in Britain. The election result gave them a majority of over 200 and virtually destroyed the Liberal Party, already rent by the feud betwen Lloyd George and Asquith. Many voters were influenced by the fear, too, that Labour was 'Bolshevik'.

Baldwin then formed his second administration and was faced with the question of whether Neville Chamberlain should return to the Exchequer.

He decided he should not, and offered the position to, of all people, Winston Churchill, who had just deserted the Liberals for the Tories, after originally being a Tory and deserting them! Baldwin's thinking here was that it would be better to have Churchill inside the Cabinet and use his energies there, than in the modern parlance have him as a 'loose cannon' on the Conservative backbenches.

Other names had been mentioned as well, but Chamberlain was content to take up his old appointment as Minister of Health. Chamberlain said at the time that 'I ought to be a great Minister of Health, but am not likely to be more than a second-rate Chancellor'. He was pleased that Austen, now firmly back in the Tory fold, was appointed Foreign Secretary, a position in which he was to have considerable success.

Chamberlain had to work closely with the new Chancellor of the Exchequer over his new scheme for contributory old-age pensions which was included in Churchill's controversial 1925 budget. The controversy surrounded the decision to put Britain back on the gold standard, so that she returned to the pre-war parity with gold. Churchill did this after consultation with the Bank of England, and later called the decision 'the biggest blunder' of his life because the return to the gold standard overvalued sterling in international markets and made British exports uncompetitive. Churchill also had to abandon his free trade beliefs to impose duties on silk and lace. This was to raise the revenue needed to pay for Chamberlain's pension reform.

CHAMBERLAIN AND CHURCHILL

Despite the acrimony of later years, Neville Chamberlain was able to establish a good relationship with his new colleague. He recognised at once those differences which made his own personality as different from Churchill's as it was from Stanley Baldwin's. Churchill was, thought Chamberlain, 'a brilliant creature' and 'a man of tremendous drive and imagination' but a colleague whose changes of mood and flights of fancy could stagger his colleagues. The Chancellor was subject to acute moods of depression which he called 'black dog', and in Chamberlain's view was too interested in personal glory. At the time of the 1925 budget, for example, Churchill seemed almost envious of Chamberlain's pension scheme saying, 'You are in the van. You can raise a monument'. Another colleague gave eloquent testimony about why Churchill was such a difficult man to work with. 'He was someone who laid eggs as quickly as a partridge, and like that bird, immediately went off to make a new nest if disturbed.'

The two men shared a paternal legacy which made both feel that they were carrying on the uncompleted missions of their fathers. Both felt, too (particularly Churchill), that their respective fathers had been badly let down by the Conservative Party. Churchill's father, Lord Randolph Churchill, had risen to be Chancellor, before resigning recklessly, and dying prematurely of syphilis. Churchill, like Neville Chamberlain, spent years watching an adored father dying a slow and painful death.

It is profoundly ironic, given the conflict between the two men in the 1930s that Churchill was appointed Chancellor, despite much opposition from Tories who regarded Churchill as a turncoat Liberal, at the tentative suggestion of Neville Chamberlain. But because of the bitter foreign policy differences which later divided them, it is often forgotten that the two men were Cabinet colleagues for six years (1924-9 and 1939-40). Churchill was later to write of 'twenty years of friendly relationship amid the ups and downs of politics' although in a moment of bitterness during World War Two, he called Chamberlain 'the narrowest, most ignorant, most ungenerous of men'. But this was out of character, for Churchill was always generous to political opponents however serious his differences with them, and in his obituary speech, he paid tribute to Chamberlain's 'perfect sincerity'.

THE GENERAL STRIKE

As a leading member of the Baldwin Government, Chamberlain found himself involved in the events surrounding the General Strike of May 1926. This arose from the refusal of coal miners to agree to an increase in working hours and a reduction of their wages to accommodate a general review of the operation of the mines. Pits were generally running at a loss in the early 1920s, and the Samuel Commission had recommended that the Government should discontinue the subsidy to the industry (paid since the summer of 1925) until the issue of pay and hours had been settled. The miners wanted the subsidy to continue and they had the somewhat unenthusiastic support of the Trades Union Congress.

Failure to reach a settlement after negotiation with the TUC in which Baldwin and Chamberlain were prominent brought out on strike not just the miners, but also other major unions like the Railwaymen and the Transport and General Workers. Chamberlain, like his colleagues, thought that the strike was unconstitutional, and potentially revolutionary, although he avoided the wild rhetoric of Churchill who put out his own newspaper, *The British Gazette* (printers having closed down the national papers) and went round breathing fire and brimstone against the strikers.

Once the strike was on, Chamberlain only played a limited role in events, although Baldwin sought his advice. But he did oppose the demand by some colleagues like Churchill that punitive anti-union legislation should be enacted *during* the srike. This fact is important because some historians have accused Chamberlain of an anti-working-class bias during the General Strike. In reality, he described the Chairman of the TUC Pugh as 'a very moderate decent fellow' and had considerable respect for the TGWU leader Ernest Bevin.

Once again, however, Chamberlain's inability to suffer fools gladly may have counted against him. He was frustrated by the way some union leaders skated around issues (although he didn't suspect them of dishonesty), and at their inability to face up to economic realities. Conversely, the detailed injustices to which the trade unionists referred in negotiations at 10 Downing Street were of deep concern to them. And Chamberlain lacked Baldwin's ability as a mollifier.

It was in this sort of situation that Baldwin's special abilities were at a premium. He broadcast to the nation, telling the people that 'I am a man of peace', and managed to win the trust of the TUC even when its leaders were embittered by their defeat in the General Strike. Thus, the General Strike collapsed after ten days, although the miners remained on strike into the following year, before they were forced back to work.

Chamberlain's reaction to the strike was generally positive. He thought that now that the trade union movement had been defeated, it was 'the time to show generosity'. Like his colleagues, Chamberlain had talked in melodramatic terms of revolution and chaos if the General Strike were not crushed, but this is not altogether surprising. The Railwaymen's leader J.H. Thomas (a leading figure in the parliamentary Labour Party) was also alarmed by what a prolonged general strike might do and wrote of how it could 'easily have developed into a revolution'.

It is important to remember that Chamberlain's own working experience with Elliott's and Hoskins had been one of mutual respect between labour and employer, and there had never been a strike. Men of his generation and background would find a phenomenon like a general strike deeply alarming, coming as it did after earlier crises like 'Red Clydeside' in 1919, when tanks were ordered onto the streets in Glasgow against trade union demonstrators.

THE RATINGS AND VALUATION BILL

Churchill might well have envied the stamina which allowed Neville Chamberlain to push through his 1925 Ratings and Valuation Bill. Chamberlain wrote of how he had 'slaved away at it night and day till one in the morning, so that when the time came I had mastered the beastly thing'.

The measure had four main aims. Firstly, to transfer the rating powers from the old Poor Law Guardians (dating from the Poor Law of 1834) in the parishes to the 'real living bodies of today'. By this Chamberlain meant the county, borough and district councils. Secondly, to achieve a single basis for rating valuation, inclusive of income tax, instead of three or four. Thirdly, to standardise the method of assessment instead of having a network of different deductions and contradictory methods in district councils. Lastly, to keep the rating system up to date by means of a single system of five-yearly valuations.

This massive measure created a single rating authority system with uniform methods, but it aroused opposition in the Tory rural areas. Some Tory MPs complained that the Bill 'nationalised local government and seriously affected the liberties of our English country people'. What it actually did was to replace 12,000 parish officials who had operated the old Poor Law of 1834 with 648 new rating authorities, and 600 Poor Law Boards of Guardians (who appointed these officials) were replaced by 343 new regional rating assessment areas. Some Poor Law Boards of Guardians remained.

Neville Chamberlain had been interested in housing since his days on Birmingham City Council, and he now also had the opportunity to follow up that interest. By the time he left office in 1929, he had built nearly a million new houses, and put 58 slum clearance schemes into operation.

Poplarism

He only did so after a full-scale row with the Labour Party after what came to be known as 'Poplarism'. It took its name from the Poor Law Guardians

THE HAPPY DESPATCH.

Shade of Mr. Bumble (to Poor-Law Guardian). "SO IT'S YOUR TURN TO BE ABOLISHED, IS IT?"
Mr. Neville Chamberlain. "NO, NO; ONLY TRANSLATED."

at Poplar in East London, who in league with the local council, paid higher rates of Poor Law relief than those recommended by Chamberlain as Minister of Health. These high-paying councils and Boards of Guardians were invariably dominated by Labour, so the issue involved some party feuding in the House of Commons. To combat the practice of overspending, Chamberlain had secured the passage of the Guardians Default Act through Parliament in July 1926, and this led him into direct conflict with Labour councillors in Poplar who, as far back as 1921/2, had been found to have overspent to the figure of £5,000 on Poor Law relief. The district auditor then surcharged the councillors which meant that they were personally responsible for the debts and their possessions could be seized in lieu of payment of the £5,000. The councillors appealed and the dispute was dragged through the courts right up to the House of Lords. It upheld the decision of the district auditor.

At this point, Poplar Borough Council appealed to Chamberlain as Health Minister to set aside the surcharge on the councillors, which he agreed to do. But angry Poplar ratepayers challenged this decision, and took it to the High Court where the judges ruled that Chamberlain had no right to make such a decision, and quashed his order.

Chamberlain could see that the situation was becoming farcical. In 1921, the Poplar councillors had been sent to jail for refusing to pay some money owed to London County Council, and there was a danger that this would happen again, and the councillors would become Labour martyrs. He, therefore, proposed legislation to cover such a situation.

The result was the Audit (Local Authorities) Bill of 1927 which, although it allowed councillors to appeal against surcharges, provided powers to disqualify a councillor for five years if he or she had spent powers to disqualify a councillor for five years if he or she had spent public funds recklessly. During the debate before the legislation took formal shape as an act, there were violent exchanges in the House of Commons with the Labour front bench spokesman, George Lansbury. Lansbury told Chamberlain that when he had been on the Council in Birmingham 'he acquiesced in the expenditure of millions of pounds, most of which he knew nothing about'. When Chamberlain disagreed, Lansbury accused him of being in league with the auditors in Poplar.

All this followed earlier clashes when Neville Chamberlain had used the powers available to him under the Guardians Default Act to curb the spending of Poor Law Guardians in Chester-le-Street and West Ham. In the case of West Ham, he had removed the guardians altogether.

Such behaviour could be used to make Chamberlain look like a cheese-paring, mean-spirited Tory (there were not a few about) who was unwilling to provide relief to the poorest in the land. One of his biographers observes that he used the powers available to him under the Guardians Default Act 'with reluctance' and this seems in tune with his record as a health and welfare reformer. But his attitude to the Labour Party in the House of Commons may have helped to create an image of a hard-faced, uncaring minister. When Baldwin asked his Health Minister to remember he was addressing gentlemen, Chamberlain noted that, in Baldwin's view,

> I always gave him the impression . . . when I spoke in the House of Commons that I looked on the Labour Party as dirt. The fact is that intellectually, they *are* dirt.

The impression given by such an attitude was bound to be unfortunate, but it did not really represent Chamberlain's attitude to the Labour Party (he was, for example, on good terms with Labour leaders like Arthur Greenwood). Nonetheless, it represented a real personal weakness because Chamberlain, master of his brief as always, could put down individual Labour MPs with crushing retorts and this caused resentment. The contrast was with Stanley Baldwin who, Roy Jenkins recalls, went out of his way to talk to his father Arthur Jenkins, a Labour MP, for a quarter of an hour when Jenkins had just been returned to the Commons. Baldwin remembered an earlier visit to Arthur Jenkins' constituency in Wales and was happy to chat about it. The contrast with Chamberlain's perceived attitude would have been sharp.

THE LOCAL GOVERNMENT ACT (1929)

Neville Chamberlain's other great reforming measure as Health Minister followed up the work done by the Ratings and Valuation Act. The 1929 Local Government Act abolished the remaining Poor Law Boards of Guardians, and totally altered the relationship between the state and the local authorities. The powers of the Boards of Guardians were transferred to public-assistance committees in counties and county boroughs, so ending a system which, as one historians has pointed out, 'tangled hopelessly with the system of national health'. This was because the guardians had been responsible for the health and welfare of the unfortunate occupants of the workhouse. Chamberlain had finally removed this blight on British society.

Chamberlain's greatest achievement was not accomplished without a good deal of opposition from Labour, Liberals and some of his own Cabinet colleagues. His biggest problem was Churchill who wished to combine the abolition of the rate paid by manufacturers and agriculture with the abolition of the Poor Law. They contributed between £40 and £50 million out of a figure of £160 million paid in rates in 1927.

Chamberlain was unenthusiastic about Churchill's scheme, and did not accept his assurance that allowing the rate burden of manufacturers to be reduced would not adversely affect the Exchequer. Churchill allowed for a £15 million deficit which he expected by 1931 to be covered by economic growth in the period 1929-31. He could not, of course, as David Dilks points out, have foreseen the Wall Street crash of 1929 and the worldwide economic slump that followed it.

After a great deal of wrangling, Churchill and Chamberlain eventually agreed that the rate paid by manufacturers to the local authorities should only be a quarter of the general rate, while agriculture should pay more at all. Nevertheless, Chamberlain persuaded Baldwin that the local authorities should then receive a block grant from the Exchequer to make up the money lost to them in rates. He also had his way over the issue of the fractional rate, because he believed that it was vital that some link between manufacturers and local authorities should be maintained. Ultimately Churchill got his De-Rating of Industry Bill through the Commons, as did Chamberlain his Local Government Bill. But it probably cost the Tories some votes, because property owners and small businessmen's rates were put up when government block grants did not meet the shortfall in rates caused by the De-Rating Bill.

Chamberlain's last great social reform was given a tumultuous reception by the Tories in the House of Commons, and *The Times* called the eventual Act 'one of the outstanding legislative achievements of the twentieth century' and went on to say that the credit for it must be placed 'in the first place to Mr. Neville Chamberlain'.

CHAMBERLAIN'S SIGNIFICANCE AS A SOCIAL REFORMER
—

The view of *The Times* has not always been repeated by historians, sometimes because of prejudices aroused by Chamberlain's records as an appeaser in foreign policy. Even A.J.P. Taylor, who did not attack Neville Chamberlain on those grounds, chose to go along with the stereotype of him as an unimaginative businessman. While acknowledging that Neville's social reforms made a bigger impact on British life than Austen's foreign policy achievements, Taylor wrote that 'he had efficiency, clarity, resolution; qualities marred only by his unsympathetic manner'. In this way, Chamberlain's achievement of carrying through twenty-one bills out of the twenty-five he put before Parliament is somewhat airily dismissed. It is open to question whether Chamberlain's record as Health Minister suggests that he was 'unsympathetic'.

Other historians who have written biographies of Chamberlain have been more sympathetic to him. David Dilks, for example, believes that 'Chamberlain contributed more than any minister to the conception of national politics locally administered which underlies much of British government to this day'. His first biographer, Keith Feiling, endorsed this view by saying that Chamberlain's measures were 'vital for future development'.

The case against Chamberlain rests on his attack against 'Poplarism' and the implication that as Health Minister he was niggardly in the allocation of relief to the poor. But the abolition of the Poor Law undoubtedly removed much of the stigma attached to poverty. The question of the degree to which Neville Chamberlain helped to alleviate it also demands examination of his record as Chancellor of the Exchequer (see p 54).

The social historian, Eric Hopkins, while acknowledging that Chamberlain's 1929 Act ended the Poor Law Administration, makes the point that 'this change in administration made little difference from the point of view of the unemployed'. After 1920, unemployment was never less than a million and the fate of many unemployed people who were deemed able-bodied was that they could not obtain poor relief.

Conversely, the 1929 Act did undoubtedly rationalise an absurdly confused situation, as Dilks points out. In one Poor Law Institution in a rural area the inhabitants consisted of 'seven acutely sick persons, 55 infirm and senile, six epileptics, eight certified lunatics, 18 certified mental deficients, nine uncertified mental deficients, one able-bodied man and three healthy babies'. Instead Chamberlain had substituted one single health authority for each area responsible for all the variety of medical services.

Essentially, therefore, the student is left with this problem. Was Neville Chamberlain a remorselessly efficient administrator who lacked compas-

THE BOO PREVIOUS.

Scene: *Theatre Royal, St. Stephen's. Première of the new Problem play "Derated."*

Manager Neville Chamberlain (*addressing hostile demonstrators in the Press Gallery after the opening scene*). "GENTLEMEN, I ADMIT THAT THIS PLAY IS UNEXCITING AND DEMANDS EXCEPTIONAL INTELLIGENCE IN THE AUDIENCE; BUT IF YOU'LL SIT IT OUT PATIENTLY I CAN PROMISE YOU A HAPPY ENDING."

sion, or was he a committed social reformer intent on raising standards of living and improving the living conditions of the people? On his housing achievement alone, Neville Chamberlain has some claim to be placed in the second category.

THE 1929 ELECTION

Stanley Baldwin confidently expected to win the election of 1929 and had been considering how to reshape his government. Indeed he had already made a crucial change by persuading Douglas Hogg, later Lord Hailsham, to become Lord Chancellor so removing a potential Prime Minister to the House of Lords. Unwittingly, therefore, he had assisted Neville Chamberlain's rise to the top although Chamberlain was on record as saying that he had no ambition to be Prime Minister. Hogg had been very popular with Tory backbenchers.

When the election came, it was a re-run of 1923, except that Labour was now the largest party with 287 seats to the Conservatives 261 and the Liberals 59. Chamberlain rejoiced at the downfall of Lloyd George (never in fact to hold office again after 1922) but felt that his own Cabinet career might be over. This was because he expected Labour to win another more conclusive election victory in two years which would keep the Tories out of office until 1936 when Neville Chamberlain would be 67 years old. He put the Conservative election defeat down to years of 'ceaseless propaganda' amongst the working class, to the effect that nothing would be right until a Labour government was elected. Chamberlain could not, of course, have foreseen the worldwide economic crisis of 1929-31, which was to bring down Ramsay MacDonald's second Labour government.

Key factors in the Government's defeat were actually the issue of unemployment, and the sending out of higher rates bills just before the election for which Baldwin's Government got the blame. An interesting feature of the campaign was that for the first time the so-called 'flapper girls', that is women between 21 and 30 years, had the vote.

Points to consider

1) Assess Neville Chamberlain's record as a social reformer.
2) Define what you understand by the term 'Poplarism'.
   Assess Chamberlain's handling of this issue.
3) Why was the Local Government Act of 1929 so important?

6

CHANCELLOR OF THE EXCHEQUER

THE CAMPAIGN AGAINST BALDWIN

The loss of a second election by Stanley Baldwin in 1929 encouraged a whispering campaign against him within the Conservative Party. Chamberlain's biographer, H. Montgomery Hyde, writes of this campaign:

> The movement was to escalate, more perhaps to Neville Chamberlain's embarrassment that to Baldwin's since Chamberlain, though coming more and more to be acknowledged in the Party as the heir-apparent, was too loyal to Baldwin to entertain any design to supplant him.

Chamberlain's diary comments at the time *seem* to support this analysis. 'Heaven knows,' Chamberlain wrote, 'I don't want the job.' Again the anti-Lloyd George theme reasserted itself as he added, 'I would not on any account play Lloyd George to his Asquith.'

Chamberlain did tell Stanley Baldwin about the complaints against his leadership immediately after the election defeat, but then departed for East Africa (Kenya, Uganda and Tanganyika, or Tanzania as it is known today). There, Chamberlain picked ip the imperialist themes of his father with a reference in a speech to the Empire forming 'a trusteeship for the backward races'. He also thought that the three territories should form an East African Federation, but this never came to pass.

On his return, Neville found that the campaign against Baldwin was still going at full blast. Austen appeared ready to join in and wrote of how he and his half brother 'are driven nearly to despair by SB's ways'. To irritation with Baldwin's lackadaisacal leadership style was now added a real issue – India. Baldwin believed, like Chamberlain, that India should be allowed to move slowly towards self-government and dominion status within the British Empire (like Australia, Canada and New Zealand). Churchill did not, left the Shadow Cabinet, and began a vigorous campaign against the whole idea that British rule in India could end in the foreseeable future. He was supported against Baldwin by the influential Press Lords Rothermere (who owned the *Daily Mail*) and Beaverbrook (who owned the *Daily Express*). Rothermere went so far as to tell Neville Chamberlain that only if Baldwin went, and he became leader, would the Press Lords continue to give one hundred per cent support to the Conservative Party. Neville Chamberlain reacted cautiously to this suggestion, believing that any move to get rid of Baldwin must be started in the House of Commons.

In Opposition, he had been asked to take over the role of being Party Chairman and here he also found Baldwin's relaxed style of leadership a problem. Baldwin was quite capable of cancelling meetings suddenly without letting colleagues know, and on one celebrated occasion, failed to make a short appearance in a film about Disraeli after claiming that he had strained a ligament in his foot during his sleep! Neville Chamberlain remarked rather sarcastically, 'Any ordinary mortal would have telephoned to save me going round to his house, but the poetic temperament doesn't work that way'.

Clearly Neville Chamberlain, like other cabinet colleagues, reached the point where he thought Baldwin ought to retire as Prime Minister, and he told Baldwin so. At one point, Baldwin told him that he would meet Shadow Cabinet colleagues the next day and tell them he was going to retire, only to change his mind.

Two factors saved Baldwin; the by-election in the St. George's Division of Westminster, and the issue of India. The first-named event was caused by the death of the sitting MP who had been anti-Baldwin, and his replacement as Conservative candidate by Duff Cooper, a supporter of the Prime Minister. Although Rothermere and Beaverbrook put up their own anti-Baldwin Tory candidate, Duff Cooper won by 5,000 votes.

Some tension was caused during the campaign between Baldwin and Chamberlain, when it became known that Baldwin intended to make a personal intervention in it. This was a breach of normal practice and Chamberlain was angered that as Party Chairman, he had not been consulted first. At a subsequent meeting Baldwin apologised saying, 'It would hurt me, if I felt a shadow of misunderstanding between us.'

At the same time, Baldwin gained prestige because Lord Irwin (his appointee as Viceroy of India) gained a considerable success by persuading the Indian leader Gandhi to call off his campaign of civil disobedience against the British and come to the Round Table Conference on India in London in 1931. These two successes saved Baldwin, and gave him the encouragement to fight on as Conservative Party leader. He showed his fighting spirit in a notable speech which attacked Rothermere and Beaverbrook for interfering in politics:

> What the proprietorship of these papers is aiming at is power, and power without responsibility – the prerogative of the harlot throughout the ages . . . this contest is not a contest as to who is to lead the party, but as to who is to appoint the leader of the party.

Chamberlain's role

The account of Chamberlain's role in the events of 1931, and the attempt to get rid of Baldwin is not as straightforward as his biographers have generally suggested. Ostensibly Chamberlain was the loyal party man, unwilling to challenge his leader. But historians have presented other evidence which rather challenges this version of events.

A key event was to the so-called Topping Memorandum presented to Chamberlain by the then Tory Chief Agent (in charge of the selection of parliamentary candidates). This said that the constituency membership was all against Baldwin and that he had to go. Roy Jenkins writes of the document:

> This document, which was rich in wounding phrases, was by no means unwelcome to Chamberlain, particularly as it ended with a fairly clear hint that he ought to be the new leader. He then behaved somewhat unctuously, showing it to half the Shadow Cabinet in order to get their advice on whether or not he ought to worry Baldwin with it.

According to Jenkins, Chamberlain then sent the memorandum to Baldwin just as he heard the bad news about the Press Lords candidate in the St. George's by-election. It is hard to square this account with Chamberlain's own declaration that 'I don't want the job'.

Baldwin's other biographers Middlemass and Barnes are less condemnatory and record the fact that before sending the Topping Memorandum around to Baldwin, Chamberlain had deleted 'a couple of phrases which he thought "too wounding"'. But they do refer to the meeting between Baldwin and Chamberlain when Baldwin told the Party Chairman that he had 'decided to go down fighting' and might even fight the by-election himself. Chamberlain allegedly replied, 'S.B. you can't do that.' Baldwin replied, 'Why not?' and got the answer, 'Think of the effects on your successor.' Baldwin saw immediately, say Middlemass and Barnes, 'that Chamberlain's attitude had not been wholly disinterested and he said curtly, "I don't give a damn about my successor." '

Both these versions of the events surrounding the delivery of the Topping Memorandum suggests that Chamberlain's behaviour during the leadership crisis was not as disinterested as he subsequently maintained. This in itself was not particularly shocking. Politicians are ambitious, and Neville Chamberlain would in 1931 have attained a position which neither his father nor his half-brother had ever achieved – leadership of the Conservative Party.

More interesting perhaps is the question of what would have happened subsequently if Neville Chamberlain had replaced Baldwin in 1931. Would Chamberlain have been content to remain in the background, as Baldwin did, in the National Government that was formed shortly afterwards? His record suggests not, but any judgement must be linked to some extent to the view taken of Chamberlain's behaviour in the leadership crisis. Further reflection on it must await the definitive second volume of Professor Dilks' biography of Chamberlain.

As it was, Stanley Baldwin could look back on 1931 as the year 'when my party tried to get rid of me'.

THE ECONOMIC CRISIS

Stanley Baldwin's battle for survival in 1931 was soon to be overshadowed by the events surrounding the economic crisis and the fall of Ramsay MacDonald's second Labour Government. Like the governments of all the western democracies, MacDonald's government seemed paralysed by indecision when traditional economic politics failed to ameliorate the slump and rising unemployment. By 1931, the unemployment figure had climbed to 2½ million.

The complete loss of confidence in the financial system by the middle of July 1931 also meant that in Britain, £33 million in gold and a further £33 million in foreign currency holdings were withdrawn from the City of London.

In the moment of crisis, Ramsay MacDonald (according to some versions) put out feelers towards the Conservatives for a national coalition but Chamberlain and Baldwin were at one in rejecting such overtures.

Throughout the crisis, Baldwin was adamant in his refusal to contemplate the idea of coalition with Labour and the Liberals. His line was that Labour had got the country into the mess, so they could get it out again. His memories of participating in the Lloyd George coalition also made him unenthusiastic about coalitions in general.

Neville Chamberlain's attitude altered as the crisis worsened. He foresaw 'a panic in the City, a hundred million deficit in the Budget, a flight from the pound, and industry going smash'. In such a situation, Chamberlain believed, Ramsay MacDonald would not be able to rely on support from his own Labour Cabinet colleagues, and would then approach Baldwin for a coalition or national government to be formed. Chamberlain was to become the leading advocate of a national government on the Conservative side. Conversely, Baldwin was unconvinced by the argument for such an alliance.

THE MAY COMMITTEE

Labour's immediate answer to the crisis facing it in 1931 was to set up the May Committee, chaired by a leading civil servnt, to recommend cuts which were supposed to balance the Budget. Philip Snowden, the Labour Chancellor, was a very traditional economist who had ignored the more radical approach of the young Labour minister, Oswald Mosley (who then left the Labour Party before ultimately founding the British Union of Fascists). When the May Committee reported, it recommended some £78 million in cuts which was to include 10 per cent of the existing unemployment insurance benefit fund, something which was certain to split the Labour Party.

MacDonald was also told by London bankers that part of the problem was political because of the 'want of confidence' in His Majesty's Government'. This would prevent the Labour Government getting a desperately needed loan in either New York or Paris.

Nevertheless, when Baldwin and Chamberlain went to see MacDonald and Snowden, Chamberlain felt obliged to support Labour in the 'national interest'. Snowden proposed to introduce a supplementary Budget and an Economy Bill, and asked for Conservative and Liberal support.

Yet again, Chamberlain was frustrated by Baldwin's apparent lassitude in such a crisis. 'He had,' complained the Party Chairman, 'apparently given no thought to the situation, asked no intelligent question, made no helpful suggestion and indeed was chiefly anxious to be gone before he was "drawn into something".' And indeed he soon was gone, back to France for the holiday which had been interrupted by the crisis facing Labour! It is only fair to Baldwin, however, to record the view of another of his colleagues who believed that Baldwin *had* formed a view of the situation. This was that the Conservatives could support MacDonald once his economy proposals were accepted by the Labour Cabinet. However, it is true that Baldwin left Chamberlain to mind the shop once more as he went off to France.

When Snowden and MacDonald went along with the May Committee and recommended cuts of £78½ million, Chamberlain thought their action courageous and worthy of support. But he also insisted that a 10 per cent cut in dole money should form part of the cuts package. This was, in part at least, because he suspected that this would prove too much for most of the Labour Cabinet to swallow. There is a flavour of rather mischievous glee about a reference in a letter to a colleague when Chamberlain said that the dole money issue would cause Labour to 'be irrevocably split'.

On Baldwin's return from France, another meeting was held with the Labour leadership, at which Herbert Samuel, the Liberal leader, was also present. In it, MacDonald said that although he would stay on as Prime Minister to get the emergency financial measures through the House of Commons, there was no point in his joining a national government because he would not have the backing of his party. Chamberlain then intervened and put it to MacDonald that although his party might not support him, the country would. Curiously MacDonald maintained that people might suspect him of clinging to office for the large prime ministerial salary. Chamberlain replied (equally curiously) that if he could persuade some of his Labour colleagues to come into coalition with him, 'the odium at least would be spread'. More pointedly, he asked what effect MacDonald's resignation would have on foreign opinion. This caused MacDonald to ask for time to reconsider. Again, Chamberlain had dominated the discussion, and one of Baldwin's biographers has complained of his 'manipulations' of MacDonald and Snowden. Was Chamberlain primarily motivated here by the national interest or a realisation that the economic crisis could be used to destroy Labour? It is difficult to entirely refute the suggestion that there was an element of seizing party advantage. Yet it was Chamberlain, rather than

Baldwin, who agitated for a cross-party administration rather than a purely Conservative one.

THE FORMATION OF THE NATIONAL GOVERNMENT

Ultimately MacDonald, urged on by King George V, agreed to lead a national government. There is some dispute about whether Baldwin agreed to join it after Samuel had persuaded the King of the virtues of coalition, or because he saw that there was no alternative.

As Chamberlain foresaw, Labour was eventually shipwrecked by the dole issue, although some Labour ministers were equally infuriated by the message from New York bankers that no loan would be forthcoming unless the economies had the backing of the Bank of England and the City. This was regarded as dictation by bankers and split the Labour Cabinet.

The National Government had Ramsay MacDonald as Prime Minister, Baldwin as Lord President of the Council (a post which did not carry special departmental responsibilities) and Neville Chamberlain as Minister of Health once more. Austen Chamberlain became, not Foreign Secretary as he wished, but First Lord of the Admiralty, which infuriated him. He told Hilda that after thirty years at the centre of affairs, 'it is not easy to adjust oneself to the position of the fly on the wheel'. Baldwin had to agree to Austen's demotion to accommodate Labour and the Liberals, both of whom had four representatives in the new Cabinet (a Liberal was Foreign Secretary).

Baldwin's seemingly minor post hid the realities of power in the National Government. For the Conservatives were by far the largest component of the coalition, especially as most of the Labour Party had deserted MacDonald when he agreed to become Prime Minister. Only a few Labour men like Snowden and J.H. Thomas agreed to serve under MacDonald whose real authority was (as he himself had feared) seriously undermined.

However, appearances were kept up precisely because Baldwin was happy just to be Lord President of the Council, and did not claim one of the big offices of state. In the view of the historian Stuart Ball this was important because *a note on . . .*

THE POLITICS OF THE NATIONAL GOVERNMENT

The National Government was formed in 1931 to deal with the economic emergency which had brought down Ramsay MacDonald's second Labour Government (1929-31).

An election was held shortly after its formation which resulted in a massive National Government majority over Labour and part of the Liberal Party. The National Government was largely Conservative, although National Labour (the small Labour remnant) and the National Liberals were represented in the Cabinet. The argument over free trade caused some National Liberals to leave the Government in 1932, although some Liberal representation remained. Thus, the National Government faced throughout its life an opposition consisting of those Labour MPs (most of the party) along with Liberals who opposed its policies. This life effectively ended in 1935 when Ramsey MacDonald retired from the premiership, and Baldwin replaced him as leader of an overwhelmingly Conservative administration, which then won a conclusive election victory. There continued, however, to be a few National Liberal and National Labour MPs in the Government until the general election of July 1945.

under no other Conservative leader would the National Government of 1931 have been possible. Baldwin's willingness to sit back and leave formal power to Ramsay MacDonald may have been the result of laziness and lack of resolution, but without it the National Government would hardly have lasted more than a few months.

National Labour (as MacDonald's supporters became known) found Lord Hailsham (Douglas Hogg) so obnoxious that they refused to serve with him in any capacity, but they did not object to Neville Chamberlain. Chamberlain's analysis of the crisis had proved to be exactly correct, because MacDonald had become the prisoner of the Tory Party. This fact was confirmed in the general election of 27 October 1931 when the

Conservatives won 473 seats, and National Labour and National Liberals combined managed only another 38 seats (Lloyd George and his supporters refused to support the National Government as did a second group of Liberals under Samuel when MacDonald said he would introduce tariffs). The mainstream Labour Party, which now regarded MacDonald as a traitor, got a mere 52 seats.

While Neville Chamberlain had been a dominant influence in the formation of the National Government, Ball may well be right in his conclusion that only Baldwin could have kept the Conservatives in the coalition for the next four years. Had Chamberlain been leader, as he very well might have been after the campaign against Baldwin earlier in the year, it is probable that a 'doer' like him would have demanded one of the great offices like the Exchequer and therefore upset the balance keeping the National Government together.

TARIFF PROTECTION

The dominance of the Conservatives in the National Government after the 1931 election meant that they could demand a larger share of Cabinet posts. Neville Chamberlain did become Chancellor of the Exchequer (Baldwin retaining the post of Lord President); there were nine other Conservatives to the five for the National Liberals and four for National Labour.

As soon as he was in the post, Chamberlain was faced by that great 'family issue', tariff protection. Neville had doubted his capacity to be Chancellor earlier in his career, as we have seen, but his stewardship of the Treasury early in the life of the National Government got this testimony from the then Liberal leader, Herbert Samuel:

> Neville Chamberlain, on the other hand, was always ready to take the lead, particularly on economic questions which then held the field and which had always been his special province. His ideas were positive and clearcut; he was tenacious in pursuit of them, whether in the Cabinet itself, or its Committees, or in the conversations that, as in all governments, were continaually proceeding among its members. Courteous and agreeable in manner, Chamberlain was willing to listen to arguments with a friendly spirit – but a closed mind.

In fact, Chamberlain had no special expertise in economic matters when *a note on . . .*

TARIFF PROTECTION AND IMPERIAL PREFERENCE

The Chamberlain family were especially associated with the campaign for imperial preference and tariff protection from the time Joseph Chamberlain resigned from Balfour's Government in 1903.

Protectionism meant abandoning the free trade system which had operated in Britain since 1846, and placing tariffs on foreign imports to protect British industries. Only in 1932 was protection formally adopted in Britain, although free trade had begun to be abandoned before this.

Imperial preference was supposed to go hand in hand with tariff protection. Its highpoint came at the Ottawa Conference of 1932 when a system of partial Imperial preference was introduced whereby Britain exempted some imports, mainly food and raw materials, from tariffs while the Dominions gave preference (in the sense that they lowered tariffs on British goods) to British exports to them. Imperial preference did, in fact, bring about an increase in trade between Britain and the Dominions (on Commonwealth) so that British imports from the Dominions rose by 25 per cent between 1930 and 1938. Exports from Britain went up from 37.5 to 45.6 per cent over the same period.

The events of 1932 showed that free trade (which had lost Baldwin the 1923 election) was no longer the sacred cow of British politics. Chamberlain's 1932 move to protection and the Ottawa Conference, forced Snowden, the former Labour Chancellor of the Exchequer, and the Liberal Free Traders out of the National Government Cabinet.

he was briefly Chancellor in 1923, and had then spent five years as Health Minister. But someone certainly needed to 'take the lead' in the circumstances facing the National Government in 1931–2. When he did so, Chamberlain was invariably convinced that he was right, and others were wrong, to the extent of suggesting inflexibility. Hence, Samuel's complaint about 'a closed mind'.

Both Baldwin and Chamberlain were concerned about the rising levels of unemployment, and the Conservative Party generally now favoured protection more wholeheartedly than it had done in either 1923 or 1929. Characteristically, Stanley Baldwin preferred to leave the detailed formulation of a tariff policy to Chamberlain and Walter Runciman, the Liberal President of the Board of Trade (a figure who was to loom large at a crucial stage later in Chamberlain's career). Speed was vital because rumours abroad about the introduction of British tariffs were beginning to flood the country with cheap foreign imports. To answer the emergency, Chamberlain brought forward the Abnormal Importation Bill which immediately imposed a 100 per cent duty on 'excessive imports'. Even the Liberals, the stoutest defenders of free trade, recognised the severity of the crisis, and did not oppose the passage of the Bill through the House of Commons.

Chamberlain knew that the Samuelites (as Samuel's supporters tended to be called to distinguish them from those National Liberals who could accept Protection) would be less happy about his next proposal. This was to place a 10 per cent tariff on all imported goods, except those from the Dominions, and some other specified exceptions. There was indeed a threat of resignation from the Free Traders (who included Snowden), which was averted only because a compromise allowed a majority vote in Cabinet, instead of the usual unanimous vote.

Chamberlain's tariff proposals were put before the House of Commons on 4 February 1932, the day which he called 'the great day of my life'. An earlier reference in Chapter Three underlines how moved Chamberlain was by the occasion, and he took along Joe Chamberlain's battered old despatch box from the days when he had been Colonial Secretary at the turn of the century.

In his speech, Chamberlain explained the need for the general tariff of 10 per cent. It would help correct the deficit in the balance of payments, and the fall in the value of the pound, as well as reducing unemployment by moving 'to our own factories and fields work which is now done elsewhere'. He had, therefore, decided that from 1 March 1932, a duty of 10 per cent would be levied on all imports into the United Kingdom, excluding only those from the Dominions. Trade policy towards them would only be decided after a meeting in the Canadian capital Ottawa. Neville Chamberlain called this *seemingly* revolutionary change in policy 'a system of moderate Protection'. 'Thus,' writes one of his biographers, 'the free trade system, initiated eighty-six years before with the repeal of the Corn Laws, was ended in 1932.' It is important to note, however, that the fear of 'stomach taxes' remained, and most foodstuffs were still exempt from duties.

The End of Free Trade and the Historians

But was the end of Free Trade a revolutionary change? A.J.P. Taylor thought not in his history of inter-war Britain saying that

> the idea of Protection had long been accepted – for the sick, for the aged, for the unemployed. It was a comparatively trivial extension of this principle when ailing industries were protected also.

As to its effects on Britain's recovery in the 1930s, economic historians have been divided about whether what Conservatives called 'the great policy' (i.e. tariff protection) notably assisted it or not.

Perhaps Chamberlain's 1932 measures were more symbolic in putting an end to a sacred cow of British politics which had been overwhelmingly identified with the Liberal Party. The exclusion of the so-called 'stomach taxes' from the 1932 measures showed that Free Trade as an issue was to be a long time dying.

The Ottawa Conference

The hopes that Neville Chamberlain had for the fulfilment of his father's dream of imperial preferences centred on the Ottawa Conference in the summer of 1932. Middlemass and Barnes write that:

> To a son of Joseph Chamberlain, fresh from his triumph with the Import Duties Bill, the assembling of the nations of the Empire to bind themselves by economic union must have seemed the apotheosis of the daring dream of 1903.

But the circumstances of 1932 were quite different and the Dominions were far more concerned with their national interests rather than the imperial one. Canada, for example, depended heavily on trade with the USA, and as her premier pointed out, 'It was difficult to beat geography.' So the Conference resuled in little more than a declaration of intent (see p.23).

Ottawa did, though, provide another example of Neville Chamberlain's persistence in dragging a reluctant Baldwin into the centre of events. He insisted that the Conservative leader head the British delegation, not least because the alternative, the Labour Colonial Secretary 'Jimmy' Thomas, drank too much, was known to tell risque stories to 'prim Catholic ladies' and had recently insulted the Canadian High Commissioner in London! As was so often the case, Chamberlain had his way.

THE FIRST BUDGET

Neville Chamberlain's first Budget in April 1932 has been described as austere. His main aim was to hold adequate reserves of gold and foreign currency, so provision was made for the borrowing of £150 million to establish a new Exchequer Equalization Fund. In his Budget, Chamberlain allowed for a possible deficit of £35 million, which was to be partly made good by his 10 per cent general tariff and a new indirect tax on tea.

At the same time, Chamberlain introduced a Conversion Scheme. The aim here was to convert £2,000 million of 5 per cent War Loan (money borrowed by the British government in World War One) into 3½ per cent stock. The scheme is generally acknowledged to have been a great success. It saved £23 million for the Exchequer in the first instance, and further conversion of the War Loan in 1932 saved another £40 million.

A.J.P. Taylor allows that the War Loan Conversion was Chamberlain's 'most considerable achievement', which gave British small investors a safe 3½ per cent return at a time of severe international crisis. He is less enthusiastic about the Budget which (apart from pulling down defence spending to an even lower level than Labour had done) he regards as 'reactionary' because it reduced the level of direct taxation from 66 per cent, where it had been since the end of the First World War, to a mere 55 per cent. This benefited the middle class which had more money to spend on consumer goods; coming from a Conservative Chancellor is perhaps not all that surprising. However, the 1932 Budget was not the savage cost-cutting exercise it might have been. Chamberlain merely enforced the 5 per cent cut in police pay which had been left out of Snowden's Emergency Budget of September 1931 by accident.

THE LAUSANNE CONFERENCE

Foreign affairs now intruded into Chamberlain's area of responsibility as well. In particular there was the longstanding issue of German war reparations, fixed at the colossal sum of £6,600,000 by the Treaty of Versailles. Germany's capacity to pay had been weakened by the effects of the Wall Street crash and the subsequent slump, although not as much as the Germans made out. But by the terms of the Young reparations plan of 1928, Germany would still have been paying reparations in 1988.

Chamberlain wanted to cancel reparations altogether, and this was the proposal he and Ramsay MacDonald put forward at the Lausanne Reparations Conference in 1932. He also wanted to cancel war debts as well. This was an equally important issue because both Britain and France had borrowed extensively in the USA during the First World War. Throughout the 1920s, a the Americans had been adamant in their insistence that this money be repaid, their attitude being memorably summed up in President Coolidge's phrase, 'They hired the money, didn't they?'

The British proposal was rejected by the French at Lausanne and Germany was still required to make a lump sum reparations payment which disappointed Chamberlain. On the personal level, though the Conference had been a success, Chamberlain had been indispensable to Ramsay MacDonald who could not speak French, and got on well with both the French and German leaders. A British embassy official told Chamberlain that the French Prime Minister Herriot 'adored' him, and Chamberlain had an equally successful working relationship with the Germans although he recorded his impression that they 'especially von Papen [the then German Chancellor] are incredibly stupid'.

These facts are interesting on two levels. Firstly, because Ramsay MacDonald is generally credited with having an effective foreign policy, and Chamberlain plainly played a significant role at Lausanne. Secondly, his success with a highly educated Frenchman with a philosophical bent like Herriot, sits uneasily with the stereotype of him as a boring, narrow-minded Birmingham businessman with no knowledge of, or interest in, foreign affairs.

One other result of the adoption of protection measures in 1932 was the ultimate resignation of Snowden and the Free Traders. This pleased Neville Chamberlain who thought that their withdrawal from the National Government would make it more unified. He hoped that the acceptance of the principle of protection by the surviving members of the Government would enable it to 'develop into a National Party and get rid of that odious title of Conservative which has kept so many from joining us in the past'. This view, long held by Chamberlain (see p. 23) was one he held in common with Winston Churchill, then excluded from the National Government because of his reactionary views on India. One of Churchill's wilder remarks was 'Gandhi should be bound hand and foot at the gates of Delhi and trampled on by an enormous elephant ridden by the Viceroy'.

FURTHER BUDGETARY SUCCESS

Chamberlain continued with the same budgetary strategy during his five year stint at the Treasury. An attempt was made to keep the balance of trade in equilibrium, interest rates were kept low, income tax was reduced, while the salary cuts imposed by the May Committee on public servants were gradually restored by the Budget of 1934.

The Chancellor was confident about the future. In 1934, he told the House of Commons that: 'We have finished the story of Bleak House and could sit down to enjoy the first chapter of Great Expectations'. By 1935, he felt able to tell his colleagues that 'Broadly speaking, we may say that we have recovered in this country eighty per cent of our prosperity'. Writing later of Chamberlain's Chancellorship, the historian C.L. Mowat agreed with his optimistic prognosis. 'The National Government's financial policies,' he wrote,

> made the best of both worlds; they seemed sufficiently deflationary to restore confidence: they were in fact sufficiently inflationary to assist recovery by maintaining the purchasing power of the people.

THE PROBLEM OF UNEMPLOYMENT

One of Chamberlain's biographers has written of the period 1932 to 1937: 'Above all, unemployment steadily fell.' Statistically this was true, but the perception of Chamberlain's economic strategy was not always a positive one, even inside his own party. In high unemployment areas like the North-East, where the recession bit hardest, the rate did decline markedly but the use of the Means Test under the 1934 Unemployment Act was bitterly resented (it was used to assess the unemployed person's assets and so calculate how much dole money he should get).

TABLE I

Unemployment 1932-7 (per cent)

	1932	1937
Coal mining	33.9	14.7
Woollen and worsted	20.7	10.2
Cotton	28.5	11.5
Shipbuilding	62.2	23.8
Pig-iron making	43.5	9.8

Nevertheless, the application of the Means Test under the 1934 Act was less rigorous, and the new nationally organised Unemployment Assistance Board extended the unemployment insurance scheme of 1911 to all workers earning less than £250 per year.

Despite this, however, the scheme could not really cope with the chronic long-term unemployment in the old traditional industries of the North, even though, as Table 1 indicates, unemployment in the older industries did decline while Chamberlain was Chancellor.

His remedy was traditional – balancing the budget, trying to stimulate production, giving tax cuts to the middle classes. Younger Tories advocated more radical measures. One was Harold Macmillan, later Prime Minister but then a rebellious Conservative backbench MP for the industrial town of Stockton-on-Tees in the the North-East. Macmillan knew from personal experience of mass unemployment what it was like to give £5 to an impoverished, unemployed constituent and his recent biographer, Alistair Horne, comments on 'the government's half-hearted efforts to combat unemployment'. Were they half-hearted? Perhaps not in Chamberlain's eyes, but he did have a streak of that nineteenth-century Nonconformist rectitude which did not wish to encourage the improvident, without always recognising that long-term unemployment was not the fault of the victims. Westminster was also a long way from Teesside and Tyneside. Many parliamentarians were shocked by the condition of the 1936 Jarrow hunger marchers who walked all the way from the North East to London to demonstrate their plight.

But in the eyes of Macmillan, who had close contacts with Labour and the Liberals (unlike Chamberlain, he was also a great admirer of Lloyd George), government measures were undoubtedly half-hearted. In his 'Middle Way' Macmillan advocated measures like public schemes to clean up the environment (and provide much needed work), public ownership of the coal mines, and a National Investment Board with trade union representation. Although Baldwin was sent a copy of the 'Middle Way', Macmillan's ideas were thought too radical for the National Government.

In Chamberlain's defence, it can be said that the Keynesian methods advocated by Macmillan and others, spending public funds to stimulate growth and employment, were not overwhelmingly successful where they were applied. In the American 'New Deal' of the 1930s, for example, high levels of unemployment remained after public works schemes were introduced.

What does seem to be true was that Chamberlain and the National Government conspicuously failed to deal with deeply entrenched pockets of chronic long-term unemployment. This unemployment, as the social historian Eric Hopkins points out, was linked to poverty. Hopkins concludes that although

> there was less grinding poverty than before the First World War, and poverty of all kinds had been considerably reduced . . . poverty in itself still remained a serious social problem; and unemployment and low wages were together responsible for more than half of it.

Neville Chamberlain was never unsympathetic to the plight of the poor, but concentrated unduly perhaps on the psychological effects of unemployment which deprived men of 'the courage, the spring, and the spirit which enable a man to face up to his difficulties and feel confident that he can overcome them'. The tragedy of the 1930s was that however much spring and spirit a man might have, it could not provide him with work in places like Stockton and Jarrow.

THE HEIR APPARENT

By the summer of 1935, it was clear that Ramsay MacDonald's health would not permit him to carry on as Prime Minister, and that he would be succeeded by Stanley Baldwin. When MacDonald resigned, Chamberlain not only kept his post as Chancellor but at last got No. 11 Downing Street as his official residence (normally the Chancellor's home). Baldwin had previously lived in it as Lord President of the Council to make up for the low salary that job carried.

Even before MacDonald's resignation, Chamberlain was, in his own words, 'carrying this government on my back'. He was also the leading figure in the Conservative Party, combining the post of Chancellor with that of Chairman of the party's Research Department. In Cabinet, too, Chamberlain invariably took the lead as one Cabinet minute laconically recorded. 'At Mr. Baldwin's request, Mr. Chamberlain opened the proceedings, *as usual* [author's italics]'. He was obviously earmarked to succeed Baldwin.

FOREIGN POLICY AND DEFENCE

Increasingly, too, Neville Chamberlain was a major player in the formulation of defence and foreign policy. His influence was clearly at work when Baldwin became Prime Minister in June 1935, when he secured the removal of Lord Londonderry as Air Minister, whom he regarded as unsatisfactory.

Later chapters deal with the evolution of the appeasement policy under Chamberlain in 1937 and 1939 (see p. 69), but as Chancellor he was bound to have a decisive input in decision-making about defence costs. He himself wanted to spend more resources on schools and hospitals, but was forced because of the European and Far Eastern emergencies to accept the allocation of some £1,500 million to defence in the years after 1935.

His involvement in comittees about Imperial Defence meant that Chamberlain was very well briefed on defence and foreign policy matters. His mastery of his domestic briefs and his predisposition to believe in the power of rational argument, may have disposed him to treat foreign leaders like badly behaved trade unionists (it was not perhaps a coincidence that his foreign policy adviser when he was Prime Minister had been the Government's chief industrial adviser).

THE ABDICATION CRISIS

Towards the end of his lengthy term as Chancellor, Neville Chamberlain was a central figure in the Abdication Crisis which ended with the formal resignation of the Crown by Edward VIII in December 1936. During the crisis Chamberlain was seen, depending on the viewpoint, at his best or worst. Indeed, some of his comments, notably one about how the failure to resolve the question of the King's marriage was damaging 'the Christmas trade', seem absurd or even pompous. His comments were not motivated by religious attitudes, as Chamberlain had long since lost his Christian faith, but by a desire to preserve the position of the Crown, and the decencies of ordinary life as perceived by a man who had after all been over thirty years of age when Queen Victoria died. Like others, he had awaited the new reign anxiously when George V died in 1935, and hoped that Edward VIII would 'pull his socks up' (a reference to the new monarch's fairly riotous social and personal life). Chamberlain being Chamberlain, he was bound to be concerned when he learnt that the King was not reading state papers as religiously as his father had done. He was also the author of a memorandum about the way the King dressed, as well as his tendency to make off-the-cuff remarks in public (the most famous being 'something must be done' to unemployed miners in South Wales). Baldwin decided it would be more tactful to suppress the memorandum.

When Edward VIII did eventually abdicate to marry the American divorcee, Mrs Wallace Simpson, Chamberlain was full of admiration for the way Baldwin had handled the crisis. 'S.B. as I anticipated,' he wrote to Hilda, 'has reaped a rich harvest of credit which has carried him to the highest pinnacle of his career.' At least one of Baldwin's biographers has doubted whether Neville Chamberlain would have handled the crisis so deftly. He, Roy Jenkins writes, 'obviously thought the King should be dealt with more like the Poplar Board of Guardians.' Alternatively he 'would have alienated the country by treating the King like a negligent Town Clerk of Birmingham'. This is not entirely fair. Part of Baldwin's success in resolving the crisis was due to the fact that, to his Foreign Secretary's horror, he wilfully neglected foreign policy to concentrate on it. Neville Chamberlain might well have felt, not without reason, that more haste would have allowed attention to have been given to more important business than the Abdication.

Issues to consider

1) **Examine Chamberlain's role in the campaign against Stanley Baldwin in 1931.**
2) **Why was Chamberlain's 1931 Tariff Bill so important?**
3) **In what ways was Chamberlain's management of the British economy open to criticism between 1931 and 1937?**
4) **How valid do you think that Samuel's remarks about Neville Chamberlain having 'a closed mind' was?**

7

CHAMBERLAIN AND APPEASEMENT

I believe that the double policy of rearmament and better relations with Germany and Italy will carry us safely through the danger period.

Neville Chamberlain

Neville Chamberlain has become permanently associated with the word appeasement, which in the post-war world has been regarded as a policy of cowardice and surrender. His reputation has suffered so much that both his foreign policy and the term appeasement need re-evaluation. One historian has gone as far as to suggest that 'appeasement' should be dropped from the language and never used by scholars, because the word has been so consistently misinterpreted. The fact remains that appeasement, in Professor D.C. Watt's words, has acquired the 'status of a myth – loaded with implication, undertones and overtones'. It has become what sociologists call a 'booword', full of negative symbolism.

The first point, therefore, to remember is that there is nothing ignoble about appeasement. To 'appease' means to conciliate, to listen to your opponent and try and meet his grievances. This was the pre-war understanding of the word, before it began to have such unpleasant overtones. How it came to have another, more sinister meaning is part of Neville Chamberlain's story and part of his tragedy.

CHAMBERLAIN AND FOREIGN AFFAIRS

Neville Chamberlain came to the premiership in May 1937, confident about his ability to run Britain's foreign policy. Some have argued that he was overconfident and lacking in experience but this is unfair. For throughout his period as Chancellor of the Exchequer, Chamberlain had been closely involved in the evolution of Britain's defence and foreign policies. His views on defence strategy carried great weight in the debates about it in the House of Commons in 1934-5, and he had strong views on foreign policy issues. He made, for example, a decisive intervention in the discussion about applying oil sanctions against Mussolini's Italy in 1935 saying that it would be 'the very midsummer of madness' to apply them. This had been done, Chamberlain subsequently remarked, because someone needed to give the lead which 'the Party and the country needed'.

Later, such behaviour was described as arrogant, but that was not the judgement at the time. Instead, the contract between Chamberlain's 'hands on' approach to foreign policy was contrasted with that of his predecessor, Stanley Baldwin. Baldwin, after all, had declared that one of the pleasures of his retirement would be that he 'wouldn't have to meet any more French statesmen' (although curiously he always spent his annual holiday at the French spa town of Aix-le-Bain). Foreigners generally mystified him, and during the Abdication crisis of 1936, he asked Foreign Secretary Eden not to bother him with foreign affairs. (The abdication of Edward VIII apparently seemed far more important to him than the fascist threat (see p. 67)).

By contrast, especially with historians who have found Chamberlain's involvement in foreign affairs meddlesome and arrogant, Anthony Eden rejoiced at Chamberlain's appointment. Before it took place, Eden confined to a friend that he and Chamberlain were 'closer to each other than to any other member of the Government'. Eden also felt that Chamberlain 'had the makings of a really great Prime Minister if only his health held out' and that 'he has a grip of affairs which Stanley Baldwin never had'. In the light of this statement, it is hard to see where the myth about Chamberlain's ignorance of foreign affairs came from.

Chamberlain also had a clear line on the related area of defence policy. He had read the books of the great military historian and theorist Basil Liddell-Hart, and agreed with the writer's view that Britain must avoid getting involved in another large-scale land war. Instead, Britain should concentrate on building up her navy and, especially, her air force, in order to deter any attack from Europe. This was classic 'blue water' strategy, like that of Palmerston or Pitt, and it was derived from personal experience as well as economic realities. Chamberlain well remembered the letters he had received from his cousin Norman who had died in the First World War, pleading with him to work to prevent such ghastly slaughter from ever happening again. His horror of war, like that of many contemporaries, was perfectly genuine.

CHAMBERLAIN AND FASCISM

Another central myth about Chamberlain is that he admired the dictators and based his dealings with them on approval of their policies. In the 1930s, the Labour Party leader, Clement Attlee, had said that 'the reason Neville truckles to the dictators is that he admires their principles'. Surprisingly, a similar statement appeared in a 1991 biography of Chamberlain's second Foreign Secretary, Lord Halifax.

Both are nonsense. Chamberlain was to describe Hitler as 'half mad' and capable of 'mad dog' acts and for years, too, his closest adviser in the Treasury, Sir Warren Fisher, was strongly anti-Nazi.

Mussolini was regarded differently only in so far as Chamberlain hoped that he could be used to try and moderate Hitler's behaviour. But even Winston Churchill had said that he would have supported Mussolini had he been an Italian, and the usually canny Lloyd George had been bewitched by Hitler when he had visited him in 1936. The myth that Chamberlain's foreign policy was influenced by the fact that he sympathised with the dictators is just that, a myth.

CHAMBERLAIN AND THE FOREIGN OFFICE
—

Chamberlain has been accused of bypassing the Foreign Office, and running his own foreign policy.

This is a fair comment. It was because he had no confidence in the Foreign Office's ability to conduct foreign policy in the manner he thought best. Very early on in his premiership, Chamberlain was to write to his sister, 'But really that F.O.! I am only waiting for my opportunity to stir it up with a long pole'.

The stirring with the 'long pole' involved bringing in his own foreign affairs adviser who was not a member of the Foreign Office; this caused great resentment. It also meant using Cabinet members other than the Foreign Secretary for foreign policy initiatives. In 1937, for example, he sent Lord Halifax (later Foreign Secretary himself in February 1938) to Germany to talk to Hitler when Eden thought he should have gone. This in itself nearly caused a diplomatic 'incident' when Halifax almost gave his hat to Hitler, whom he mistook for a footman. Another farcical situation arose when Halifax returned. Eden complained about Halifax's encouragement of German claims and Chamberlain testily told him to go home and take an aspirin. His handling of close colleagues could sometimes be insensitive.

This incident has often been blown up to show how arrogant and insensitive Chamberlain was. In reality, it demonstrates how Eden could also be a bit of a prima donna who, to quote a recent study, 'lived on his nerves', and was annoyed because Halifax rather than he had been to see Hitler.

Of course, Chamberlain *was* in error in not going through official channels. But he was not the only Prime Minister to try and run his own foreign policy. Eden himself did so in 1955-6, ignoring all contrary advice, and telling all and sundry that he wanted Colonel Nasser, the Egyptian leader, to be overthrown during the Suez Crisis. So, latterly, did Margaret Thatcher. Yet Chamberlain, more than others, has been castigated for ignoring Foreign Office advice.

CHAMBERLAIN AND APPEASEMENT
—

Although there was continuity between Baldwin's foreign policy and Chamberlain's, there was also a distinctive flavour to the latter's. Baldwin's policy had been one of 'wait and see', one perhaps which suited his personality and essential lack of interest in foreign affairs. This involved *reacting* to events rather than making initiatives, and Chamberlain wanted a more positive stance.

This was partly at least because as Chancellor of the Exchequer, Chamberlain had worried about the cost of rearmament, and the way the arms race was affecting the programme of domestic reform in which he so much believed, and had been such an effective agent of as health minister.

If, Chamberlain reasoned, diplomacy could bring about an understanding with the fascist dictatorships, and so lessen the arms bill, this was a goal profoundly worth striving for. Given the choice between 'guns or butter', Chamberlain would invariably have opted for butter, and his strategy was not an ignoble one. His belief was that if the burden of arms spending became so heavy that it endangered Britain's economic recovery (still at a delicate stage after the Depression), then a diplomatic solution had to be found. In his mind, therefore, economic viability, rearmament and diplomacy were all part of the same strategy. They had to be kept in balance with one another so that the country would be secure in its defences, yet economically viable. To understand this is to understand the so-called 'new appeasement' which Neville Chamberlan is accused of masterminding because he failed to perceive the Nazi threat. Unlike Baldwin, Chamberlain had a coherent programme which allowed foreign policy initiatives to be made. It was light years away from the traditional stereotype of a 'silly old man with a brolly' which has littered many post-war history books.

THE EMPIRE

Children in pre-war British geography lessons were very familiar with the image of a globe with one quarter of its surface painted pink to represent British colonies/possessions. But the very size of the British Empire posed enormous defence problems. The Statute of Westminster of 1931 had also recognised the self-governing status within the British Empire and Commonwealth of Australia, South Africa, Canada, New Zealand and the Irish Free State.

The Irish Free State wanted nothing to do with imperial defence, and in South Africa, the Afrikaners were hostile to British interests. The same was true of the French Canadians, and in Palestine, Egypt and India there were *a note on* . . .

TERMS AND CONCEPTS

Appeasement: normally meaning the process of listening to an opponent in an effort to redress his grievances by negotiation. Appeasement as applied by Neville Chamberlain during his premiership allegedly moved away from classic appeasement, by betraying the national interest in attempting to negotiate with Germany and preserve the peace.

Chamberlain spoke of his 'double line' which meant negotiating with both Germany and Italy while building up Britain's armed strength. This was necessary, according to Chamberlain, because Britain was in too weak a position in 1937-8 to challenge the Axis powers.

The term **New Appeasement** has sometimes been used about the period March 1939 to September 1939 when Chamberlan gave guarantees of assistance to Poland, Turkey, Rumania and Greece. This apparently more foreceful policy was still combined, however, with attempts to redress German grievances by peaceful negotiation. It can also be used about the whole Baldwin-Chamberlain policy in the sense that their appeasement policy was dictated by perceived military weakness rather than strength. **Classic appeasement** would ideally be negotiation from *strength*, which allows reasonable concessions to be made to an opponent (Britain and France followed such a policy in the 1920s in signing the Locarno Treaty (1925) and allowing Germany to enter the League of Nations (1926)).

nationalist movements which wanted the British out. In India, the British were, perhaps, fortunate that Gandhi was a pacifist and urged his Congress movement to protest non-violently. An armed revolution in India would have presented the British with insoluble problems. Of those whose loyalty could be most heavily relied upon, Australia and New Zealand (quite naturally because of their geographical location) regarded Japan as the greatest threat to the Empire.

Always in Chamberlain's mind as well was the global nature of Britain's commitments and her consequent vulnerability. Thus, appeasing the dictators in Europe was also a result of the recognition that imperial Japan was a threat to British interests in the Far East. These could not be protected adequately if Britain was drawn into a conflict in Europe, as what happened in 1941 (when Japan overran Britain's Far Eastern colonies) demonstrated only too clearly. So in the Far East a policy of appeasement and bluff was the order of the day, most ably carried out by Sir Robert Craigie, the British Ambassador in Tokyo. The nightmare scenario here was that the Anti-Comintern Pact (1936) binding Germany, Italy and Japan together against Communist Russia would be turned into a formal alliance against Britain and France. Fortunately it was not, but Japan (especially after her invasion of China in 1937) was as much of a rogue elephant in the Far East as Germany was in Europe. It is too easy, therefore, to condemn Chamberlain's appeasement of Hitler by ignoring the fact that Britain's military resources were overstretched, and that he knew this to be the case.

THE USA

—

Another factor in the equation was the likely attitude of the United States, which had isolated itself from European affairs in 1919. Chamberlain never put much faith in the hope of American assistance, but he believed that it was important to show the Americans that Britain had done everything possible to preserve the peace. This effort was acknowledged when President Roosevelt sent Chamberlain a two-word telegram after the Munich conference had staved off war in 1938. It said, 'Good man'.

THE USSR

—

If Chamberlain had little faith in American help, he had even less desire to ask for Russian help or to believe it was necessary. In common with many fellow Conservatives (and many other political leaders), Chamberlain did not trust the USSR, and did not want an alliance with it. His predecessor, Stanley Baldwin, was on record as saying that he hoped 'the Bolshies and the Nazis' would knock hell out of one another.

Chamberlain certainly had some sympathy for the view that Nazi Germany could be a bulwark against communism, but we cannot deduce from this that he was in any way pro-Nazi. Nor did he see Nazism or Italian fascism as the lesser of two evils. But this rejection of the USSR as a potential ally did put a heavier burden on the Anglo-French alliance, and France certainly felt that her share of the military burden was unduly heavy. This was not surprising as, by 1938, Britain could only promise to put two army divisions in the field as against France's ninety.

The aversion to communism also meant that Chamberlain was led into blind alleys where defence policy was concerned, saying, for example, that Poland was 'a great virile nation' that would be a more useful ally than the USSR (only, it should be stressed, after March 1939 when he had to review his policy). He tended to write off the value of the Red Army as a fighting force but this wasn't entirely his fault, first of all because Stalin's purges of that army in 1937-8 did damage it, and secondly, because the British military attaché in Moscow kept sending back a stream of very pessimistic (exaggeratedly so) reports about its condition. Chamberlain also believed that Stalin was trying to embroil the western democracies in a war with Germany, to the benefit of the USSR. Anti-appeasers pointed out that Chamberlain's animosity to the USSR *predisposed* him to accept such bleak estimates at their face value.

Where defence policy was concerned, appeasement meant 'limited liability' in Europe. Britain would defend France and Belgium against aggression, as she was bound to do by the Locarno Treaty of 1925, but no more than that. She had no commitment to new states like Austria or Czechoslovakia, and Chamberlain's brother Austen had said that Eastern Europe wasn't 'worth the bones of a British grenadier'. The Prime Minister agreed with these feelings entirely. He relied on the great French army to deter Germany on the continent with minimal help from its British counterpart. Meantime, efforts would be made to defend the British heartland by building up the RAF, but without damaging the recovery of the British economy.

This, then was the policy of appeasement which Chamberlain formulated and followed until it became untenable in March 1939. It was a policy derived partly from Britain's military weakness and overstretched resources, but also from Chamberlain's determination not to abandon his programme of domestic reforms. Schools and hospitals were to have the same priority as Spitfires and Hurricanes.

CHAMBERLAIN'S CRITICS

At the time, criticism of appeasement within Chamberlain's own Conservative Party was muted. His chief critic was Winston Churchill, something of a rogue elephant by 1937 because of his views on India and the Abdication crisis, whose small band of followers included Tory MPs like Brendan Bracken, Harold Macmillan and Robert Boothby.

Churchill accused Chamberlain of betraying Britain's national interest by encouraging Hitler's aggressive demands, notably at the Munich Conference of September 1938 (see p.97) and the events leading up to it. At Munich, Churchill argued £1 was demanded at the pistol's point. When it was given £2 was demanded at the pistol's point. Finally, the dictator consented to take £1.17.6d and the rest as promised for the future'.

Churchill recognised some of Chamberlain's difficulties, realising for example that the Air Ministry were giving the Prime Minister inaccurate figures about the RAF expansion early in 1938 (so that Chamberlain wrongly told the French that Britain was building 350 aircraft a month). The true figure Churchill noted 'was only ½', a fact which he himself made known in the House of Commons so that Chamberlain was annoyed with the Air Ministry. This Churchill 'ought to make Neville think. He does not know the truth; perhaps he does not want to'.

Churchill was also critical of Chamberlain's dismissive attitude to the League of Nations whereas he wanted 'a renewed, revivified, unflinching adherence to the Covenant of the League of Nations'. Interestingly, although as Chancellor in the 1920s, he had presided over big arms cuts, Churchill did not share his leader's preoccupation with the need to raise people's standard of living. For him, defence took priority and he watched uneasily as Germany's armed strength grew. He did not hold Chamberlain entirely responsible for this, however. Rather the 1938 situation, said Churchill, was the result of 'five years of futile good intention. Five years of eager search for the line of least resistance, five years of uninterrupted retreat of British power, five years of neglect of our air defences'. In another memorable phrase Churchill described the period 1933-38 as 'the years that the locust hath eaten'.

Churchill had no truck with the idea that Germany could be appeased by giving away the territory of smaller nations. It was wrong, he believed, for any State to give up 'one scrap of territory just to keep the Nazi kettle boiling' or for Britain to bully such a small State into doing so. Concessions to Hitler, Churchill and the anti-appeasers believed, would encourage further German territorial demands and the only way to circumvent Hitler was to rearm at breakneck speed. By contrast Neville Chamberlain was 'oppressed with the sense that the burden of armaments might break our backs' (although he never denied the need for rearmament).

Precisely because they believed concessions from weakness would be fatal, Churchill and the anti-appeasers were firm advocates of the French alliance and a wider network of anti-German alliances (see p.91). They felt that Chamberlain did not cultivate strong ties with France (this was a valid point because he was dubious about the French government's reliability) and put too much faith in negotiation with Germany and indeed Fascist Italy. Chamberlain, as we have seen, was dubious about foreign alliances even before he went into politics.

Both Baldwin and Chamberlain found Winston Churchill a nuisance on the defence issue. He bombarded them with statistics, made doubly irritating by the fact that many of them had been obtained from sympathisers in the Air Ministry and the Foreign Office! Although Chamberlain instituted enquiries to find out who those 'moles' were they never got anywhere.

THE LABOUR PARTY
—

Labour had no coherent critique to offer either. They deplored Chamberlain's appeasement policy and accused him of fascist sympathies, but consistently voted in the House of Commons against plans to build up the armed forces. How was Hitler to be stopped without armed strength? This was a question Labour was never able to answer, and its faith in the League of Nations proved to be an illusion. Chamberlain himself never had any faith in it, and neither did he believe that his opponents had a valid case. The 'double line' as he called it of 'rearmament and better relations with Germany' would serve Britain best until she was in a stronger position.

Chamberlain's appeasement policy was shaped in the recognition of Britain's commitments and resources. His critics may have argued that Chamberlain did not give sufficient priority to the fascist threat, but they could not show that the Prime Minister had opposed rearmament. The debate was really about the *pace* of rearmament, which Chamberlain was reluctant to accelerate. This was precisely because he was a man of peace who wished to improve the living standards of his people. So when confronted with the threat from Nazi Germany, Chamberlain preferred (in the first instance) to conciliate, and use diplomacy to try and meet German grievances. This policy was an expression of a natural preference *and* a recogniton that Britain had severe military weaknesses. It had nothing to do with cowardice or betrayal of British interests because Chamberlain's own armed forces chiefs were telling him precisely that. Britain could not, and should not, fight a war against Germany (and possibly Italy and Japan) because she was not strong enough to do so. In spite of the fact that he accepted the advice of professional soldiers, sailors and airmen, Chamberlain rather than they has been labelled as a defeatist.

CHAMBERLAIN AND THE NATIONAL INTEREST
—

Another argument ran parallel with the debate about appeasement. This concerned the nature of Britain's national interest, and rival perceptions of it. On the one side were the advocates of the 'balance of power' school of international relations who thought that Britain must fight to prevent any one power from dominating the continent of Europe, just as she had done in 1588 against the Armada and in the nineteenth century against Napoleon. Even in 1914, when Britain had apparently gone to war to save Belgium, she was really fighting to prevent Germany from dominating the continent. And in the 1920s, some members of the British establishment thought they needed to prevent France dominating the continent.

The rival school, of whom Chamberlain was one, did not fear German domination in Eastern Europe, and even regarded it as natural. His ambassador in Berlin, Neville Henderson, for example, who had the Prime Minister's full support, warned against 'jealous objections to German economic and even political predominance in Eastern Europe'.

This view derived in part from the feeling, widespread in Britain after 1919, that Germany had been harshly treated by the Versailles Treaty. It had been ably expressed by the great economist, John Maynard Keynes, in his *Economic Consequences of the Peace* and remained a potent influence. Chamberlain himself thought that National Socialism was a direct consequence of German resentment against the harsh peace treaty, and that German grievances should be listened to with understanding. Although fully committed to defending France and Belgium from attack, therefore, he did not regard Eastern Europe as a vital British interest. Neither, as we have seen, did his brother when he was Foreign Secretary in the 1920s. But when Germany broke peace treaties, Neville Chamberlain pushed ahead with the rearmament programme.

This difference of perspective was to show up most noticeably during the Czech crisis of the summer and autumn of 1938. Chamberlain described Czechoslovakia as a 'faraway country of which we know nothing' (while Churchill on the other hand, following the 'balance of power' approach, described the loss of its territory as 'a total unmitigated defeat *for Britain*). This statement has brought much abuse down on Chamberlain's head, but it almost certainly represented majority opinion in Britan at the time, just as Queen Mary's remark about fighting for 'tiresome Serbia' had done in 1914. Yet, ultimately, Britain did not fight for Serbia or even for Belgium. Chamberlain's belief, therefore, that she should not fight for Czechoslovakia was not so outrageous as it has been made out to be by some, both at the time and since 1945. Czechoslovakia was not a vital British interest for Chamberlain or for the heads of his armed forces. For Churchill and his supporters it was, because, in their view, one surrender to German demands would encourage others. But it was Churchill who was out of step with British policy after 1919, which had not regarded the Eastern European territorial settlement as Britain's business.

The argument about the national interest, therefore, was a finely balanced one. In a sense *both* views of it were right, because although Britain had avoided entanglements in Eastern Europe, since 1919 there was also a strong case for standing up to Hitler after Germany made its intentions clear. As it turned out, the flow of events would make the *revisionist* view (those, who like Chamberlain who would revise Versailles and be sympathetic about German grievances) untenable.

THE AIR MENACE

Any discussion of appeasement also needs to take the climate of public opinion into account, which in the 1930s, was profoundly anxious about the threat from the air. It was, after all, Stanley Baldwin who had said that 'the bomber will always get through'.

This fear was largely a matter of ignorance, as no one really knew what the effects of large scale aerial bombing would be. But it was heightened by films like *Things to Come* (1936) with its shots of terrified civilians running for shelter in their gas masks, and the real life bombing of the Spanish town of Guernica in 1937 by German planes participating in the Spanish Civil War. To all this was linked the assumption of Germain air superiority, based on what we now know to be quite false figures. The Germans were adept at producing propaganda which exaggerated their own air strength.

Fears about gas proved to be quite illusory as the Germans never used it, but it was widely assumed that gas bombs would be dropped in the event of war, based on the use of gas during World War One. Chamberlain reflected this particular fear in a broadcast during the 1938 Czech crisis (the same one with the reference to 'a faraway country') when he spoke of how incredible and horrible it was that British civilians were having to try on gas masks. He also knew about the extraordinary weakness of Britain's anti-aircraft defences in 1938 when there were just twelve anti-aircraft guns to defend the whole of London. Neither, at that stage, did Britain have radar or Spitfires in any numbers.

There was a sense, of course, in which the exaggeration of German air strength *played into* the hands of the appeasers. This was because it allowed them to argue that German air power was so great that the RAF couldn't take it on (it is a paradox that by talking up the German air threat, Churchill allowed this to happen, when he did have a strong case for further rearmament.) But this was not the core of Chamberlain's argument. He believed that appeasement would allow German demands, many of which were regarded as being not unreasonable, to be met, thus removing the need for massive rearmament. He also, as outlined above, was determined to promote Britain's economic recovery and this meant keeping down defence spending. Nevertheless, the sixty-nine year old Prime Minister was alarmed by the sight of London's defenceless streets when he flew to meet Hitler in Germany in 1938. Although the bomber would not 'always get through', the fear that it might was still a significant factor in Chamberlain's thinking in those immediate pre-war years.

THE TREASURY AND THE DEFENCE CHIEFS

The divided Empire was paralleled by divisions in Whitehall. The chiefs of the armed services believed, on the one hand, that Britain could only win a long drawn-out war in which the resources of her empire could be fully mobilised.

The Treasury held exactly the opposite view, believing that the fragility of the British economy after the Depression would make it possible to fight only a short war. Somehow or other, Chamberlain, himself a former Chancellor, had to evolve a policy out of all these complex and contradictory factors.

THE MEDIA

A neglected area of the Chamberlain partnership until recently has been the relationship between the Chamberlain Government and the media. Chamberlain was rather a good performer on contemporary newsreels, and for a man born in the Victorian era, he had a keen appreciation of the value of radio broadcasts. It is known that pressure was put on the BBC on Chamberlain's instructions so that anti-appeasement talks or those likely to upset the Germans were cancelled, or so rescripted that they became innocuous.

A recent study by Richard Cockett has also shown how Chamberlain, through his press office at No.10 Downing Street, attempted to 'muzzle' the British press and make it toe the appeasement line. Ambassador Henderson in Berlin (a firm Chamberlain ally) was persistent in his demands that the British newspapers should not offend Nazi sensitivities; and he had a good deal of success, not an especially helpful development in a democracy.

Chamberlain certainly had a powerful ally in Geoffrey Dawson, the Editor of the *Times* newspaper which was then regarded abroad as the mouthpiece of the British Government. Dawson remarked that he stayed awake at night worrying about whether anything in his paper might offend Hitler's government!

Media manipulation demonstrated the rather authoritarian bent behind Chamberlain's appeasement policy, because as a critic observed, 'he thought he was right'.

THE HISTORIANS

Increasingly since the 1960s, historians have come to be more sympathetic to Chamberlain's difficulties. One of them, P.R. Schroeder, has written:

> If one begins to tot up all the plausible motivations for
> appeasement . . . one sees that these are far more than enough to
> explain it. It was massively over-determined . . . any other policy

in 1938 would have been an astounding, almost inexplicable divergence from the norm.

Others have argued that there continues to be a strong argument against Chamberlain's policy, but there is no longer a place for an out and out rejection of appeasement, because of the sheer complexity of the problems facing the British Government in the late 1930s.

The great historian A.J.P. Taylor turned the whole argument on its head by stating that Chamberlain did not carry appeasement far enough, and holding Britain and France rather than Germany largely responsible for the outbreak of World War Two. 'The only thing,' wrote Taylor, 'wrong with Hitler in international relations was that he was a German.' This theory was unusual in its attemp to push Chamberlain forward as an initiator of events, rather than Hitler. Most historians disagree and still regard the war that started in September 1939 as essentially 'Hitler's War'. They see Chamberlain's policy as essentially a response to perceived threats to British interests. One, Edward Ingram, sees Taylor's attempts to explain the events of 1938-9 as essentially *nationalistic*, because Britain was for him the centre of the world: 'He is the quintessential patriotic historian, pining for nineteenth-century triumphs.'

Neville Chamberlain did not pine for triumphs but for peace, and the circumstances in Europe in 1938-9 were to make its attainment impossible.

THE MEANING OF APPEASEMENT

Before reading about the actual events which faced the Chamberlain government in 1938-9, it is important not to confuse the term appeasement with what it came to mean for Chamberlain's opponents in 1938, and to accept its intrinsic value.

There is nothing, therefore, intrinsically evil about appeasement or in seeking 'patiently and faithfully for peaceful compromise' as Churchill remarked. The difficulty lies in getting the balance right between appeasement and endangering the national interest. Some historians like Richard Lamb and many contemporaries of Chamberlain, have felt ultimately that he did not.

Points to consider

1) Discuss what you understand by the term 'appeasement'.
2) Suggest ways in which Neville Chamberlain's conduct of foreign affairs was different from his predecessor's.
3) Outline the factors which made Chamberlain's foreign policy choices so difficult.
4) What do you understand by the term 'the national interest'? How did Chamberlain's view of it differ from Winston Churchill's?
5) What did Chamberlain mean by the phrase 'the double line'?
6) How did Chamberlain's experience as Chancellor of the Exchequer influence his foreign policy making?

8

THE EUROPEAN CRISIS 1938–9

We cannot foresee the time when our defence forces will be strong
enough to safeguard our trade, territory and vital interests against
Germany, Italy and Japan at the same time.

Report by the Armed Services Chiefs, December 1937

Any evaluation of Chamberlain's appeasement policy centres around his
handling of the three great crises in Central Europe in 1938-9. An
examination of these crises allows us to examine the themes mentioned in
the last chapter in their historical context.

THE ANSCHLUSS

Austria was a small state which had been created by the Treaty of Saint
Germain in 1919. It was a rather sad remnant of the old Habsburg Empire
which had occupied most of Central and Eastern Europe before 1914, and
was in constant economic and political difficulty after the war. In 1934, for
example, there was a workers' uprising in Vienna, which was crushed with
some brutality by the forces of the right-wing dictator Dollfüss. Shortly
afterwards Dollfüss himself was assassinated by Austrian Nazis, and
German involvement in the murder was suspected. Thereafter Austria
existed in an uneasy relationship with its giant neighbour, symbolised by the
1936 Austro-German 'Gentleman's Agreement' which legalised the
Austrian Nazi party once more, and granted trading concessions to
Germany.

Austria was not a vital British interest, and the British Government
foresaw the possibility that Hitler, an Austrian by birth, would wish to unite
Austria with Germany (although in 1931 Britain had joined France's protest

against a planned Austro-German customs union). Nevertheless, Article 80 of the Versailles Treaty did ban *anschluss* or union between Austria and Germany.

THE ROOSEVELT INITIATIVE

Even before the Austrian crisis burst in February-March 1938, Chamberlain was involved in wrangling because of the distinctive nature of his foreign policy. He did not, as we have seen, expect much in the way of assistance from the USA, and was probably surprised in January 1938 when President Franklin D. Roosevelt (US President 1933-45) made an initiative suggesting that a world conference should be held about existing problems. Chamberlain did not doubt American goodwill or their respect 'for international obligations' but doubted whether President Roosevelt could really make a positive intervention in European affairs. This view was not unreasonable. Roosevelt was bound by Neutrality Acts which the US Congress had passed, and could not offer armed assistance, even if he personally was anti-fascist.

So Chamberlain, later accused by Eden and Churchill of missing a great chance of enlisting US help, was probably right to reject Roosevelt's proposal. His ambassador in Washington wrote about 'rampant isolationism' in the USA, and Chamberlain noted how it was 'still impossible for America to stand outside Europe and watch it disintegrate'. As this was *exactly* what the USA did do between 1938 and 1941, it seems unfair to criticise Chamberlain for his caution over Anglo-American relations.

Chamberlain versus Eden

The other point about the so-called 'Roosevelt initiative' was its significance in the on-going struggle between Chamberlain and Eden. Eden was on holiday when Roosevelt's proposal came in, and Chamberlain dismissed it without telling him. This angered Eden and brought on the resignation which meant that when the highpoint of the Austrian crisis came, the Foreign Secretary had been replaced. Again the issue was partly linked to Chamberlain's tendency to go over Eden's head about foreign affairs. In this case, he agreed to have a meeting with the Italian ambassador alone, and when Eden found out about it, he insisted on being present. But the real argument was more serious. Eden wanted to be tougher with Italy than with

Germany, and asked for the removal of Italian troops from Spain where they were helping the Nationalist rebels fight the Republic. The Italian ambassador refused to agree to this proposal and Chamberlain, according to Eden, became angry about the latter's antagonism towards Mussolini, accusing him of 'missing chance after chance' of getting on better terms. What is certain is that Chamberlain believed that Eden's personal antagonism towards the dictators in general had stopped him from improving relations. He also thought that Eden did not share his conviction about the paramount need to avoid war, and that in the end his resignation was inevitable. 'I have never felt a doubt,' Chamberlain wrote, 'that it was now or never if we were to avoid another Great War.'

During the course of the interview with Chamberlain and Eden, the Italian Ambassador Count Grandi had said that Italy was worried about German meddling in Austrian affairs. Superficially, this seemed true, because in 1934, Mussolini had rushed troops up to the Italian-Austrian border to show his displeasure when Dollfüss was murdered. But in reality, the Italians had told Hitler that they regarded Austria as being part of 'a German problem'.

In this situation there was little that Chamberlain or his government could do. In February, Hitler had sent for the Austrian Chancellor von Schuschnigg and bullied him into allowing a Nazi supporter into his cabinet. Bravely, Schuschnigg had gone home and called a plebiscite to ask the Austrian people whether they wanted union with Germany or not. Chamberlain thought this action provocative, and his new Foreign Secretary, Lord Halifax, had already noted that Germany seemed 'set head-on to achieve its aims in Central Europe'. When Hitler sent German troops into Austria over the weekend of 11-12 March 1938, Chamberlain felt that this move 'had to come' and it appeared to have the approval of the Austrian people, who gave Hitler a ninety-nine per cent 'yes' vote when he held his own plebiscite.

Thus, although in public the British government deplored German action, which had broken the Versailles Treaty, it had long given up hope of protecting Austrian independence. So, too, had the French. For Chamberlain, like many of his colleagues, Austria was a German-speaking land which properly belonged to the German Reich. He might dislike the way the Germans went about their business, but in the case of Austria, the logic of language and culture pointed to *anschluss* as the logical solution. There was, too, the burden of the unjust treaty which needed to be righted. The British, in the words of the deputy editor of *The Times*, were 'bound by our sins right back to the peace treaty'. In this sense, the Anschluss of March 1938, although illegal in international law, was seen in Whitehall as a form of natural justice. Only when the British case against Germany was, as Sir Neville Henderson said, 'copper bottomed' would strong action be justified. The German annexation of Austria did not, in Chamberlain's mind, justify armed action by Britain even supposing it had been possible. Neither Britain nor France was willing or able to safeguard Austrian independence.

THE CZECH CRISIS

Like Austria, Czechoslovakia was a creation of the 1919 peace settlement. But unlike her, Czechoslovakia was a stable western-style democracy, with an alliance with France dating from 1924. The founding father of the Czech state, Thomas Masaryk, was one of the great figures of inter-war politics, who
died in 1935 just before his creation was endangered.

The Sudetenland

Czechoslovakia's problem was its minorities. These included Poles, Hungarians and, most significantly, three million ethnic Germans living in a frontier area called the Sudetenland. In the years of prosperity before the Depression of the 1930s, there was little sense of tension in the Czech democracy. But, ominously the Depression bit hardest in the Sudeten German areas. No one, however, could accuse the Prague government of real discrimination against minorities, as a minorities law gave generous protection to the rights of the different racial groups in Czechoslovakia.

The British position with regard to Czechoslovakia differed from that adopted over Austria only in the sense that France's commitments to the Czechs were recognised by Chamberlain and his colleagues. Otherwise, Britain had no commitment to Czechoslovakia other than the general one given to all member states by the League of Nations Covenant. The 1925 Locarno Treaty, which Britain had signed, made no statement about safe-guarding the borders of the East European states. The nature of Britain's commitments were spelled out by Neville Chamberlain in a speech in the House of Commons on 24 March 1938, some two weeks after the Anschluss:

His Majesty's Government have expressed the view that
recent events in Austria have created a new situation
to which consideration of these events has led us. We
have already placed on record our judgement upon the
line 5 action taken by the German Government. I have nothing
to add to that. But the consequences still remain.
There has been a profound disturbance of international
confidence. In these circumstances the problem before
Europe, to which in the opinion of His Majesty's Govern-
line 10 ment it is their most urgent duty to direct their
attention, is how best to restore this shaken confidence,
how to maintain the rule of law in international affairs,
how to seek peaceful solutions to questions that continue
to cause anxiety. Of these the one which is necessarily
line 15 most present in many minds if that which concerns the
relations between the Government of Czechoslovakia and the
German minority in that country, and it is probable that
a solution of this question, if it could be achieved,
would go far to re-establish a sense of stability over
line 20 an area much wider than immediately concerned.
Accordingly, the Government have given special
attention to this matter, and in particular they have
fully considered the question whether the United
Kingdom, in addition to those obligations by which she
line 25 is already bound by Covenant of the League and the
Treaty of Locarno, should, as a further contribution
towards preserving peace in Europe, now undertake new
and specific commitments in Europe, and in particular
line 29 such a commitment in relation to Czechoslovakia.

Chamberlain's statement is interesting from a number of perspectives.
Firstly, it contains a *public* rather than a *private* response to the Anschluss.
His Majesty's Government deplored German action, but had long realised
that there was nothing effective it could do in response. Secondly, it raises
the issue of the relationship between the Czech government and its Sudeten
German minority which, strictly speaking, was none of Britain's business.
Lastly, Chamberlain refers to the question of whether Britain should make
'a commitment in relation to Czechoslovakia'. Such a commitment would

mark a complete repudiation of the foreign policy Britain had adopted since 1919.

Unsurprisingly, Chamberlain concluded that it would not be in Britain's interest to make such a commitment to Czechoslovakia, because a guarantee of help would put Britain's policy in the hands of the Czechs. Who could know if Czech refusal to negotiate about the Sudeten Germans, who were now demanding self-government, might not lead to war beween Germany and Czechoslovakia? If Britain gave a guarantee she, too, would be dragged into such a war. Ultimately, Chamberlain was not prepared to pay such a price to protect the unity of the Czech state.

But he did recognise that the independence of Czechoslovakia might be in danger, especially after what had happened to Austria. The British Government was well aware also that Hitler's stated aim in *Mein Kampf* was to bring *all* Germans, native-born or otherwise, inside the frontiers of the Third Reich. It was Czechoslovakia's misfortune to have three million people of German extraction living inside her frontiers.

This danger was acknowledged later in Chamberlain's speech of March 24 which also stated that, if war came, 'It would be quite impossible to say where it might end and what governments might become involved.' This was a coded warning to the Germans about what an attack on the Czechs might mean.

Just in case there's any mistake

At the same time, Chamberlain had looked at the possibility of helping France if she was called upon to help the Czechs, under the terms of her 1924 Treaty. Britain could not, he said, promise France such help because to do so would again bind her to the policies of the Czech Government. If they brought France into a war,, then Britain would (if she gave such a guarantee) have to follow. Nor could Britain promise to preserve Czech independence by armed force if they were attacked.

In its way Chamberlain's speech was quite masterly. It had two quite distinct components:

1) It kept the Germans guessing about what *might* happen if they made a reckless attack on Czechoslovakia.

2) It avoided giving any kind of guarantee of assistance to the Czechs, or to the French if their treaty obligation required them to help the Czechs.

In retrospect, Chamberlain's line can appear two faced and (especially to a Czech) rather dishonourable, but it was consistent and not determined by what had happened to Austria. Back in November 1937, Chamberlain's Cabinet had already rejected the idea of giving the Czechs a guarantee in return for allowing the Sudeten Germans some form of autonomy. Chamberlain felt (and Eden agreed) that such a commitment would not be accepted by British public opinion, and was not in Britain's interest.

The Rejection of 'The Grand Alliance'

The problem with Chamberlain's statement of 24 March 1938 was its ambiguity. Could he be certain that the Germans would not call his bluff, by assuming that if Britain wouldn't offer the Czechs a guarantee of assistance, this was because she was unwilling to do *anything* at all? In such circumstances, Hitler might well be capable of a 'mad dog act', as Chamberlain feared.

Given such a possibility, the question of alternatives has to be raised. Such an alternative was provided by the Churchill, 'balance of power' school in the form usually known as 'The Grand Alliance'. This involved constructing an alliance between Britain, France, the USSR and some of the smaller states like Poland, Czechoslovakia and Rumania. It would exist under the umbrella of the League of Nations Covenant in the form of a mutual defence treaty.

This plan had an obvious appeal and Chamberlain confessed that he himself was 'much attracted by it'. But as Doctor John Charmley has pointed out, Chamberlain, unlike Churchill, was in power and had the responsibility for Britain's defences. He had, therefore, to look at the Grand Alliance proposal 'much more thoroughly and in particular get military advice on it'.

The longer Chamberlain looked at the Grand Alliance scheme, the less he liked it. The fact of British animosity to the USSR has already been touched upon in the last chapter; Chamberlain believed that Stalin was 'stealthily and cunningly pulling all the strings behind the scenes to get us involved in a war with Germany'. No one in the Tory party had any time for a Russian alliance, apart from Churchill's little group of MPs, and Chamberlain's military advisers had also written off the Red Army because of the purges of 1937-8.

This may well have been an error, as a recent study has pointed out that the Russians had earmarked 350 aircraft to fly to Czechoslovakia in the event of war, and placed as many as 17 divisions on war readiness. But Chamberlain cannot be blamed for going along with expert military advice, and this advice was that the Red Army could not be taken seriously as an 'offensive force'.

France, too, as far as Chamberlain was concerned, was a doubtful asset. Her constant changes of government suggested instability, and her defensive strategy was known to revolve around the great static fortifications of the Maginot Line. How, Chamberlain asked (not unreasonably), was France to help the Czechs while her army was to remain behind the Maginot Line? It was a fair question because France actually had no plan to help the Czechs.

ALL YOU HAVE TO DO IS TO SIT DOWN

It was also true that the right-wing parties in France hated communism, and were hostile to the treaty which France had signed with the USSR in 1935. While Winston Churchill cried, 'Thank God for the French army,' Chamberlain did not share his enthusiasm for the French alliance.

All we need to add to the equation is the extent of Britain's world-wide commitments, already referred to, and the policy of non-involvement of the USA in European affairs (see pp 75-6, 86). The Grand Alliance was an impressive concept, but its component parts seemed to be defective. It also reminded Chamberlain of the pre-war Entente which the appeasers regarded as a mistake.

None of this meant, however, that Chamberlain would renounce his commitment to rearmament. The March speech contained such a commitment, and the rearmament programme continued apace. Chamberlain's critics continued to claim that this pace was too slow.

The 'May Scare'

Throughout the summer of 1938, the demands of the Sudeten German party for self-government became more strident. The British government was unaware of the fact that the Sudeten leader, Konrad Henlein, was actually taking orders directly from Berlin and that these orders were to keep raising his demands. Henlein himself might have been satisfied with autonomy alone, but it was Hitler, rather than he, who was calling the shots.

German scare stories about alleged Czech 'atrocities' in the Sudetenland were creating an extremely tense atmosphere which culminated in the celebrated 'May Scare' during the third weekend (20-21 May) of that month. German newspaper threats against the Czech President Beneš and his government reached such a pitch that the Czechs believed that they were about to be attacked. The Czech army was, therefore, mobilised and both France and the USSR, which had pacts with Czechoslovakia, were asked for their support. This was forthcoming, as was British support for France if she was a victim of German aggression. What Chamberlain would not do, once again, was promise support for Czechosovakia if she were attacked. He was, nonetheless, very angry about German behaviour saying that the fact was

> that the Germans who are bullies by nature are too conscious of
> their strength and our weakness and until we are as strong as they
> are, we shall always be kept in this chronic state of anxiety.

This was a classic exposition of the thinking behind the 'double line', with its emphasis on building up British strength until 'we are as strong as they are'. Until then, in Churchill's phrase, 'jaw jaw was better than war war'. This was not the language of a weak-kneed, naive Prime Minister who swallowed all of Hitler's lies.

Days later, Hitler told his generals of his 'unalterable decision to smash the Czechs' which was almost certainly an angry reaction to the fact that the

THE IDES OF MARCH

John Bull. "Thank goodness that's over!"

[Pessimists predicted "another major crisis" in the middle of this month.]

Czechs had the nerve to stand up to him. In fact, the 'May Scare' was a false alarm, but the Czechs and their allies, France & the USSR, showed every sign of being willing to fight. Whether this apparent humiliation (when in fact Hitler was *not* ready to attack the Czechs) brought forward Hitler's plans to get the Sudetenland by force if need be, is uncertain. But it did underline Chamberlain's commitment to France, and if she stood by the Czechs and was attacked by Germany, British involvement was inevitable. The key question in the summer of 1938 was whether France would indeed stand by the Czechs. Chamberlain suspected that she did not intend to do so, and increasingly the French Prime Minister Daladier seemed to allow the British leader to take the initiative over the Sudetenland. The reason was simple. France could not, and would not, go to war with Germany without British support. This fact made Chamberlain, rather than Daladier, take the leading part in the negotiations with Hitler. It also made the Anglo-French side active in bullying the Czechs into accepting *their* terms, rather than the ones which President Beneš and his fellow countrymen found acceptable.

THE ROAD TO MUNICH

The month of September 1938 was to be decisive as far as the Sudetenland was concerned, and Chamberlain was to play a central role in its fate. This process really began in August when Chamberlain sent Walter Runciman, the President of the Board of Trade, to Prague on a fact-finding mission. This was a mistake because Runciman was easily hoodwinked by the Sudeten Germans into believing their atrocity stories, but the Runciman mission was yet another example of Chamberlain's penchant for circumventing the Foreign Office. It also showed how Chamberlain's anxiety about war had brought about direct British intervention in the Czech crisis, when it was France which had the formal links with the Czechs. But this anxiety, in contrast with the Baldwin period, was coupled, in the view of P.M.H. Bell, with the 'great energy and confidence' with which Chamberlain and his government took on the central role in the relationship between the western democracies and Hitler's government.

Daladier talked big, but when he and his colleagues visited London, Chamberlain subjected them to embarrassingly searching questions which revealed the fact that France was really looking around for an excuse not to support the Czechs. This only strengthened Chamberlain's belief that it was his personal task to find a solution to the Sudeten question. That he was right to take the initiative is demonstrated by the fact that on 20 July, the French Foreign Minister told the Czech ambassador in Paris that France would not in any circumstances fight for the Sudetenland.

Berchtesgaden

Early in September, President Beneš virtually conceded the Sudeten German demand for autonomy, but Hitler was not prepared to settle. On 12 September, Hitler made a threatening speech at Nuremburg, and at the same time, there was anti-Czech rioting in the Sudetenland. In Chamberlain's view, there was a grave danger of war at this point, and he decided to fly to Germany to meet Hitler in person. This, despite the fact that at sixty-nine, he had never flown before in his life. But he was determined above everything to preserve the peace, and merits Bell's description of him as a leader of 'great ability, drive and courage'. The French weren't consulted first.

The meeting was held at Berchtesgaden on 15 September and Hitler demanded cession of the Sudetenland to Germany. Chamberlain agreed to put this demand to his Cabinet colleagues who agreed to plebiscites in majority German areas, as did the French. A second meeting with Hitler was arranged for 22nd September at Godesburg.

Godesburg

When Chamberlain arrived at Godesburg he was outraged to learn that Hitler, yet again, had raised his demands. Not only, said the Führer, was the Sudetenland to be evacuated by the Czech authorities by 1 October, but Polish and Hungarian claims on Czech territory were to be settled as well.

Chamberlain told Hitler that if this was his attitude there was no point in negotiating further.

Plainly, though, the Prime Minister, dismayed by the prospect of war, had second thoughts. This, in turn, dismayed his colleagues including Cadogan, the Permanent Under Secretary at the Foreign Office, who wrote in his diary that Chamberlain 'was also satisfied that Herr Hitler would not go back on his word once he had given it'. The historian Richard Lamb, who is sharply critical of Chamberlain's behaviour at this time, notes:

The inner group of the Cabinet which had been firm in Chamberlain's absence, with the Prime Minister present, turned round in favour of capitulation.

Other culprits are castigated as well including 'the Chiefs of Staff for their failure to impress on the Prime Minister that military intelligence from the French proved Hitler to be in a weak bargaining position'.

After Munich, Churchill was to add weight to this criticism by saying that the settlement undermined the position of discontented German generals who were planning to remove Hitler from power if he dared to attack Czechoslovakia.

The crucial player at this stage was Lord Halifax, the Foreign Secretary, who after a sleepless night changed his mind and decided that 'he did not feel it would be right' to put pressure on the Czechs to accept the Godesburg terms. Chamberlain had been prepared to bully the Czechs into acceptance and he was shaken by Halifax's change of heart; he wrote to the Foreign Secretary that 'your complete change of mind is a terrible blow'. Another blow was that Hailsham, the Lord Chancellor, Chamberlain's oldest Tory friend and most longstanding colleague in the Cabinet, wrote to him in the firmest possible terms saying that Britain 'could not trust Herr Hitler's declarations in future'.

Here was a crisis indeed for Chamberlain whose strongest instincts about foreign policy were now under challenge from his colleagues. But he did not change his view that Britain could not and should not fight. Crucially, he was backed by the heads of the armed services. The Army Chief of Staff said that it would be 'madness to expose ourselves to annihilation for the sake of the Czechs'.

Does this exonerate Chamberlain from responsibility? Certainly the anti-appeasers at the time could not exonerate him because for them the need to support Czechoslovakia was as much a moral issue as a military one. Chamberlain did not see the issue in this way, and for this he has subsequently been criticised, with some validity, by historians like Lamb and Gilbert and Gott. In Chamberlain's mind there was only one policy to follow in September 1938. Here this he was wrong, at least partly because he was so certain of the rightness of his own convictions.

Chamberlain's view of Hitler

It is worth noting in the light of subsequent criticism of Chamberlain's naiveté when dealing with Hitler, that his immediate reaction to meeting the Führer for the first time was to say that he looked 'entirely undistinguished' and like 'the house painter he once was' (it was a contemporary delusion in Britain that the German dictator had been a house painter rather than a failed artist). After Godesburg, he also told his Cabinet colleagues that Hitler was 'frightful' and 'the commonest little dog you ever saw'. Less creditably, after the Berchtesgaden meeting Chamberlain said that Hitler 'was a man who could be relied upon when he had given his word'. But Joseph Stalin, the ruthless Soviet dictator, was to make exactly the same mistake.

After Godesburg, war seemed to be inevitable. Air raid trenches were dug in Hyde Park, and gas masks were distributed. The Royal Navy was mobilised and the Czechs were told to go ahead with their mobilisation. French troops manned the forts of the Maginot Line.

It was at this point that Chamberlain made his remark about Czechoslovakia being 'a faraway country'. It is generally forgotten that at the outset of the Sudeten crisis, President Beneš himself had objected to Anglo-French intervention because those two countries 'were too far away to understand these things'. Yet, when Chamberlain referred to the distance between Britain and Czechoslovakia, his critics pounced on the statement as proof of his ignorance and lack of interest in Czechoslovakia's fate. In truth, Chamberlain was expressing the bewilderment of the man in the street that such a remote conflict could lead Britain into war (Beaverbrook's *Daily Express* ran a headline asking 'Where is Prague?'), and his own horror of war. He was far from being uninterested in Czechoslovakia's fate, *providing* Britain did not have to fight on her behalf. But the major additional thrust of British policy was to persuade the French not to honour their obligations either.

MUNICH
—

In his radio broadcast after Godesburg, Chamberlain made it plain that he would be prepared to fly to Germany a third time, if this would preserve the peace. He also played one of his few remaining cards, which was to ask the

Italian dictator to intervene in the crisis, and propose an international conference to resolve the Sudeten question. It was a long shot but it worked, because on 28 September, Mussolini asked Hitler to postpone his mobilisation and agree to a conference.

The circumstances in which Chamberlain received the news that Hitler had agreed were dramatic, for the invitation (from Hitler) to attend a Four Power Conference in Munich arrived as Chamberlain was speaking in the Commons. The note was passed to Chamberlain who reportedly asked his colleagues, 'Shall I tell them?' before passing on the news that he had 'been informed by Herr Hitler that he invites me to meet him in Munich tomorrow morning'. What followed can only be described as bedlam on the parliamentary benches, as MPs, both Tory and Labour, hurled their order papers into the air, amidst shouts of 'Thank God for the Prime Minister'. This exactly matched the mood of the moment, and only Churchill and his few supporters failed to join in the general rejoicing. Later suggestions that the note passing was stage managed for dramatic effect, because Chamberlain already knew of Hitler's offer, lack any real substance.

So it was that on 29 September 1938, Chamberlain, Daladier, Hitler and Mussolini met in the Bavarian capital Munich, where the Führer had started his career in inglorious fashion in 1923. The Czechs were not even invited to the conference deciding their fate, and Chamberlain has rightly been criticised for this piece of insensitivity. Neither was the USSR, leaving Stalin in the happy position of being able to claim that he would have helped the Czechs if France had honoured her 1925 Treaty (she had signed a second agreement with the Czechs in 1935, as had the USSR, but it didn't come into force unless the French stood by their treaty obligations).

The Sudetenland was rapidly disposed of by the Munich Agreement which gave the Czechs until 10 October to evacuate the area. An international commission was to determine Czechoslovakia's new frontiers, and the Four Powers were to guarantee the security of what was left of Czechoslovakia. Critics suggested that the fact that the inkwell to be used for signing the agreement was found to be dry was a comment on its dubious morality. Some historians have also certainly been outraged by Chamberlain's apparently insensitive comment on the day of the agreement (and after the wretched Czech representatives had been told of their country's fate) that he was 'pleasantly tired'. It certainly lacked sensitivity (a frequent offence by the Prime Minister), but Chamberlain's primary and almost obsessive objection was to preserve the European peace, and in this sense, the fate of Czechoslovakia was in the view of a distinguished historian, 'cruel necessity'. Critics of Chamberlain's policy also need to ask themselves when, if ever, the great powers have concerned themselves unduly with the rights and interests of smaller ones.

In this context, it is salutary to remember that in that same year, 1938, Chamberlain was instrumental in returning to Ireland those 'treaty ports' which Britain had kept when Ireland became independent in 1921. For acknowledging the rights of a small nation in this way, Chamberlain was fiercely attacked by Winston Churchill, who was also, by a historical paradox, his chief critic over Munich.

After the signing of the Munich Agreement, there was a much misunderstood sequel the next morning. Chamberlain went to Hitler's flat in Munich and signed what became known as the Anglo-German Declaration which Chamberlain read out at the airport on his return to London. It stated that:

> We, the German Führer and Chancellor and the British Prime Minister, have had a further meeting today and are agreed in recognising that the question of Anglo-German relations is of the first importance for the two countries and for Europe.
>
> We regard the agreement signed last night and the Anglo-German Naval Agreement as symbolic of the desire of our two peoples never to go to war with one another again . . .

Hitler subsequently said that he had only signed the declaration 'to please the old gentleman', but Chamberlain did so with a clear strategy in mind. 'If Hitler signed it and kept the bargain,' he told his Parliamentary Private Secretary, Lord Home, 'well and good . . . if he broke it, he would demonstrate to all the world that he was totally cynical and untrustworthy.' Chamberlain was particularly sensitive to US opinion which would see that he had fought to keep the peace and blame Hitler if he broke it. He was not Hitler's dupe.

This eminently sensible move was unfortunately neutralised almost at once by a statement Chamberlain made on his return to 10 Downing Street. He may have been momentarily thrown off balance by the frenzied, relieved crowds singing 'For he's a jolly good fellow', or the telegram from George VI telling him to go to Buckingham Palace to receive the King's 'heartfelt congratulations'. According to Lord Home, somebody inside No. 10 said something like, 'Go on, Neville, say something to the people'. So

Chamberlain did, reusing the words of Disraeli on a similar triumphant occasion in 1878, and saying that: 'This is the second time in our history that there has come back from Germany to Downing Street peace with honour. I believe it is peace for our time.' It was a statement which the Prime Minister almost immediately regretted, and contributed powerfully to the legend about the 'silly old man with a brolly' who was hoodwinked by Hitler at Munich. Chamberlain's reputation has never recovered, and the vast majority of historians have ignored the retraction he made within a week to the Commons when he put down the offending statement to 'a moment of some emotion, after a long and exhausting day'. Dramatic, off-the-cuff statements were, as Chamberlain acknowledged after the Downing Street statement, just not his style. 'I don't do that sort of thing', he told a colleague. But his lapse produced a howler which placed him in the 'every schoolboy knows' hall of historical villains.

The mood of Munich in Britain also tends to be forgotten. Cinema newsreels were lavish in their praise of Chamberlain, as, with the one exception of *Reynolds News*, was the press. He and Mrs. Chamberlain received 52,000 letters of gratitude between them, and gifts ranging from fishing rods (Chamberlain was a keen fisherman) to four thousand tulips from Holland and cases of wine from France. The King of the Belgians wrote to say, 'You have done a wonderful piece of work and done it under the guidance and providence of God.' Munich, therefore, may not have meant 'Peace for Our Time', but most of Europe shared Chamberlain's hope that it would do. If, as some historians have complained, this adulation went to Chamberlain's head, this is hardly surprising.

MUNICH IN RETROSPECT

There were groups and individuals in Britain, of course, for which the Munich Settlement was not a matter for rejoicing. Sir Robert Vansittart, for example, the Chief Diplomatic Adviser to the government, coined the slogan, 'If at first you don't appease. Fly, fly again'; a sarcastic reference to Chamberlain's three flights to Germany. In the Commons, Churchill, who had told Chamberlain that he was 'very lucky' when Hitler's offer of talks came in, told the House of Commons that:

> All is over. Silent, mournful, abandoned, broken, Czechoslovakia recedes into the darkness. She has suffered in every respect by her

association with the Western democracies and with the League of Nations . . . Many people, no doubt, honestly believe that they are only giving away the interests of Czechoslovakia, whereas I fear that we shall find that we have deeply compromised, and perhaps fatally endangered, the safety and even the independence of Great Britain and France.

Here was the crux of the matter. Whatever had happened to Czechoslovakia, and no one could deny that that country had been truncated, Chamberlain's case was that he *had* been considering the 'safety . . . and independence of Great Britain' at Munich. And the argument was finely balanced, more so than Chamberlain's critics were prepared to allow.

There was, in the first instance, the 'air menace', and the fact that in September 1938, Britain had just one squadron of Spitfires, no radar, and thoroughly inadequate anti-aircraft defences. Everyone believed, Churchill included, that the Luftwaffe was vastly superior to the RAF.

TABLE 2

	Actual German air strength August 1938		British estimates of German air strength September 1938	
	Total	Combat ready	Total	Combat ready
Fighters	643	453	810	717
Bombers	1,157	582	1,235	1,019
Dive-bombers	207	159	247	227

Chamberlain also knew that the President Roosevelt approved of the Munich Agreement, and that feeling in the British Empire was overwhelmingly against war over the Sudetenland. Rightly or wrongly, the USSR was also deemed a valueless ally for Britain, and the French had shown no disposition to fight for Czechoslovakia either. The British ambassador in Paris had told Chamberlain that 'all that is best in France is against war, almost at any price'. (This was an exaggeration, but it coincided with Chamberlain's impressions after talking to Daladier and his colleagues.)

Above all, although Czechoslovakia had its supporters, Chamberlain's policy represented the popular mood and took into account the nature of Britain's worldwide commitments. Professor Paul Kennedy, therefore, concludes that: 'Far from finding Chamberlain's policy in the late 1930s inexplicable, it now seems quite understandable to many historians.'

There is also a strong case against the Munich Agreement. The Czechs had lost their strong frontier fortifications and were now virtually defenceless. Hitler had been given a bloodless triumph and sneered at 'the little worms' (Chamberlain and Daladier) he had seen at Munich. Stalin, whatever his motives, was bound to be suspicious of Western intentions after the abandonment of the Czechs. Even the 'breathing space' argument is flawed, because although Chamberlain got another year for rearmament at Munich, so did Hitler.

Given this narrow margin of advantage, Chamberlain's defence rests in part on the evidence that, whatever Britain or France decided to do, Hitler *did* intend to fight for the Sudetenland and would have called his opponents' bluff. After Munich, he told other Nazi leaders that Chamberlain had 'spoiled my entry into Prague', and that if anyone else tried to intervene like that again, he would 'kick him downstars'. Even if Chamberlain's policy is regarded as the wrong one, it cannot be described as craven because the reasoning behind it was cogent and reasonable. Only with the value of hindsight have some historians been able to condemn Chamberlain so completely. At the time, one of the Prime Minister's chief military advisers declared that 'we cannot expose ourselves now to a German attack. We simply commit suicide if we do'. In these circumstances, it was not unreasonable to go to Munich because it seemingly served Britain's national interest. Tragically, the same journey by Chamberlain could not have been in Czechoslovakia's interests as Churchill warned. But Chamberlain's overwhelming interest too, was the national interest of Britain.

FROM MUNICH TO WAR

The record shows that although Chamberlain hoped that Munich would preserve the peace, he allowed for the possibility that it would not. However, he, like many others, could not readily accept the fact that Hitler treated international treaties like so much confetti.

But in the absence of any real response to friendly overtures to Germany after Munich, Chamberlain did reluctantly begin to consider whether the idea of 'limited liability' as far as the Army was concerned was still appropiate.

TABLE 3

Distribution of the British Army 1938

Station	Approx. Total
Home	107,000
India & Burma plus Indian Army	190,000
Middle East and Mediterranean	21,000
Far East	12,000
West Indies	2,000

Increased aircraft production meant that the RAF was rapidly catching up with the Luftwaffe, but the Army could still only send 2 divisions to France in the event of war.

Another feature of post-Munich policy was the attempt to bring Mussolini back into play as a possible moderating influence on Hitler. To this end, Chamberlain and Foreign Secretary, Lord Halifax, visited Rome in January 1939, but the results were not encouraging. Mussolini oscillated between annoyance with Hitler ('every time he occupies a country, he sends me a message'), and admiration for German strength; it was felt he could not be relied upon.

This left France, and Halifax, at least, feared that she might remain neutral in the event of a war between Britain and Germany. The Foreign Secretary therefore persuaded Chamberlain to encourage the French to push ahead with their rearmament, especially in the air where they had become weak. (Churchill nicknamed Halifax 'Holy Fox' because of his tendency to get divine approval for his sometimes foxy actions.)

Hitler looks distrustfully at the Anglo-Italian *rapprochement*

Colonial Appeasement

For Chamberlain there was a difficulty because Mussolini had his eyes on the French colonial empire in North Africa, and the French absolutely refused to make any concessions. He was prepared, like successive British governments since 1933 had been, to restore Germany's colonies which had been lost in 1919, but Hitler wasn't interested. In fact, Chamberlain went further and was prepared to offer *other country's* colonies (eg Portuguese Angola), but at no stage did Germany see the issue as anything more than a bargaining pawn. Colonial appeasement was a failure.

THE FALL OF CZECHOSLOVAKIA
—

By February 1939, Chamberlain was hopeful because there had been no more Hitlerian adventures since Munich, and British rearmament was proceeding steadily. His colleague, Sir Samuel Hoare, unwisely allowed these hopes to go to his head by referring to the hope of 'a new golden age' early in March.

Such hopes were rudely shattered on 15 March 1939 when, after bullying the Czech President Hacha into giving his permission, German troops invaded Czechoslovakia and occupied Prague. Slovakia became an independent republic under German protection, while the Czech lands to the north came under direct German rule. The impudent excuse given for German aggression was that the troops were restoring law and order.

Two days later, Neville Chamberlain made a speech in his native Birmingham which is often regarded as a crucial turning point in the history of appeasement. Certainly its tone was angry enough, as Chamberlain asked his audience whether the destruction of Czechoslovakia was 'the end of an old adventure or the beginning of a new one.' But the only really new note, prompted by Halifax, was the suggestion that at some stage Britain would be prepared now to fight to prevent further German aggression. This rather vague pledge did not stop Germany annexing Memel, a city in Lithuania with a German majority, on 22 March.

The real turning point for Chamberlain and his policy of appeasement came in rather bizarre circumstances; firstly, in response to a 'scare' started by the Rumanian minister in London to the effect that Hitler was about to attack his country, and then to a report by the correspondent of *The News*

Chronicle. This gentleman, a Mr Ian Colvin, came home with stories about an impending attack by Germany on Rumania and seems to have convinced Halifax and Chamberlain about the genuineness of his sources. In reality, Colvin was being fed scare stories by anti-Nazi elements in German military intelligence, and the Rumanian scare was equally bogus.

The Polish Guarantee

Nevertheless on 31 March 1939, Chamberlain told a startled House of Commons that if there should be any 'action which clearly threatened Polish independence', then the Poles could rely on the support of the British government. It was, as Professor Watt has pointed out, a draconian switch away from the trend of British foreign policy since 1919 because 'it left no option whatever to the British government. If the Poles took up arms, then Britain fought too'. Thus, Warsaw had been given an influence over British policy, which Chamberlain had never been willing to concede to Prague six months before. Subsequently, in an extension of the new policy, guarantees of British assistance were also given to Greece, Turkey and Rumania if they were attacked. In April, Chamberlain introduced conscription which was both a deliberate attempt to encourage France, and a concession to what had been a longstanding French demand. Britain could not expect France to stand by her, without some more meaningful commitment to French defence.

These were all sizeable changes in Britain's foreign and defence policies. But the essence of the 'double line' still remained in place after March 1939. Rearmament was in full swing, but Chamberlain still hadn't given up hope for better relations with Germany and Italy. Economic appeasement of Germany, through stronger trading relations, was still pursued but Italian behaviour was discouraging. On Good Friday, 1939, Mussolini invaded and occupied the tiny Balkan kingdom of Albania (long an object of Italian ambitions) and in May, the Duce signed a military alliance known as the 'Pact of Steel' with Germany. Plainly, this sort of behaviour by Italy very much undermined Chamberlain's hope that she would be a moderating influence on Hitler.

TABLE 4

Contemporary Estimates of Land Forces of the European Powers, 1938–1939
(strengths, expressed in divisions, are war strengths)

	January 1938	April 1939
Germany	81	120-130
Italy	73	85
France	100	100
Great Britain*	2	16
USSR	125	125
Czechoslovakia	34	–
Poland	40	40

* British forces available for the Continent

TABLE 5

Contemporary Estimates of First-Line Air Strengths of the European Powers, 1935–1939
(in numbers of military aircraft of all types)

Year	France	Germany	Gt. Britain	Italy	USSR
1935	1,696	728	1,020	1,300	1,700
1936	1,010	650	1,200	–	–
1937	1,380	1,233	1,550	1,350	–
1938	1,454	3,104	1,606	1,810	3,280
1939	1,792	3,699	2,075	1,531	3,361

Notes

1. There were no agreed definitions as to what constituted first-line aircraft, consequently estimates differed considerably.
2. Totals for France and Great Britain are for metropolitan and overseas strengths. Reserves are not included for any of the powers.

The Soviet Alliance

Now under the influence of Lord Halifax, who wished to take a tougher line against the dictators, Chamberlain was forced to look again at the concept of the Grand Alliance. But he did so without enthusiasm, particularly where Soviet Russia was concerned. It was nevertheless clear after the destruction of Czechoslovakia that the most effective deterrent against Hitler would be a military pact between Britain, France and the USSR. France already had one, although only her left-wing parties, the communists and the socialists, were enthusiastic about it. The major problem with the Soviet alliance was geography. If, for example, Germany attacked Poland, the Red Army would have to be allowed onto Polish soil and this was something the Poles would not stomach. To do so, one of their generals said, would be worse than allowing in the Germans for 'with the Germans we would lose our liberty, but with the Russians we would lose our souls'. Hundreds of years of Russian occupation had not been forgotten in Poland.

With Rumania barely more enthusiastic about the prospect of the Red Army going to Poland via their territory, a dilemma faced the Anglo-French alliance. Somehow or other, the Poles or the Rumanians had to be made to allow Russian troops onto their territory. In this process the French were to take the lead because Chamberlain's reservations about having Stalin as an ally remained. Since Munich, Stalin was also extremely suspicious about Western intentions, fearing some sort of deal with Germany.

War for Danzig

Poland, like Czechoslovakia, was a child of the 1919 Peace Settlement. In her case, the territorial settlement was even more offensive to a rabid nationalist like Hitler because a large chunk of former German territory, known as the Polish Corridor, had been given to the Poles to give them access to the Baltic Sea. At the same time, the city of Danzig with its German majority had been put under the control of the League of Nations, although the Poles had access to the port facilities. This made an enemy out of Germany, while the Russo-Polish war of 1920-21 brought about a loss of Soviet territory to Poland which meant that she had no admirers in Moscow either.

Polish policy did little to reflect these twin perils, and her seizure of the coalmining area of Teschen from Czechoslovakia during the Munich Crisis had aroused a good deal of disgust in Britain. Before March 1939 certainly, a war for Danzig and the Corridor would have been unthinkable in Britain, not least because of the authoritarian dictatorship which ruled in Poland. Czechoslovakia, at least, had been a democracy.

After the destruction of Czechoslovakia everything was different. For not only was Poland offered a guarantee in Chamberlain's March speech but in April, this had been formalised into a treaty of alliance. The Polish Foreign Minister, by now under pressure from Germany over Danzig and the Corridor, accepted the British guarantee between 'two flicks of a cigarette'.

Yet Chamberlain continued to assert that Britain was not irrevocably tied to Poland, because he would decide when her independence was in danger. Paradoxically, Chamberlain also made the exaggerated remark about Polish military virility (quoted in the last chapter) which proved, alas, to be totally misplaced. This seems to have been a clear extension of his anti-Soviet prejudice, which he claimed was justified because no one except 'our fatuous opposition' wanted a Russian alliance inside Britain. Except, of course, his *bête noire* Churchill, who continued to bombard a frazzled Prime Minister with memos about the rearmament programme!

Many historians have criticised Chamberlain for dragging his feet over the attempt to obtain a Soviet alliance, but one recent study has suggested that, once convinced of its inevitability, the Prime Minister was content. Britain, he thought, was still 'in the danger zone' and he could see no prospect of real understanding with Germany 'as long as the Jews obstinately go on refusing to shoot Hitler' (he was genuinely shocked by Nazi persecution of the Jews).

THE END OF APPEASEMENT?

Nevertheless, he continued to work for an understanding with Germany, however remote its achievement might be. In that sense, at least, appeasement had not died in March 1939. This is apparent from a letter which Chamberlain wrote to his sister Hilda in July:

> It is very difficult to see the way out of Danzig but I don't believe it is impossible to find, provided that we're given a little time and also provided that Hitler doesn't really want a war. I can't help thinking that he is not such a fool as some hysterical people make out and that he would not be sorry to compromise if he could do so without what he would feel to be humiliation. I have got one or two ideas which I am exploring though once again it is difficult to proceed when there are so many ready to cry *'nous sommes trahis'** at any suggestion of a peaceful solution.

Here is another example of how Chamberlain, a strong and decisive leader, could also be ambivalent. On the one hand, he well knew that Hitler was capable of 'mad dog acts', but on the other, he hoped that even after

* 'We are betrayed.'

March 1939, he 'would not be sorry to compromise'. This can easily be portrayed as the height of naiveté, because of what is now known about Hitler's long-term aims and objectives, but it was not all that far-fetched. In 1938-9, Hitler's attitude towards Britain was dominated by what his arrogant and stupid Foreign Minister, von Ribbentrop ('von Brickendrop' as he was nicknamed in Britain after gaffes like giving George VI the Nazi salute when he was the ambassador there) told him. This advice was that the British were feeble and weak and would never fight. Had Hitler been advised differently, he may (we can't put it any higher than that) have tailored his foreign policy accordingly.

Chamberlain, pre-eminently a man of peace, continued to hope that Hitler could be persuaded to see reason, but the pace of the rearmament programme (see Table 4) showed that he never put all his eggs into that particular basket.

THE NAZI-SOVIET PACT

All hopes for a Grand Alliance collapsed on 23 August 1939 when Germany and the Soviet Union signed a non-aggression pact. A secret clause provided for the partition of Poland between Germany and the USSR. Chamberlain, like almost everyone else in Europe, was dumbfounded. How had anti-Marxist Nazi Germany come to sign such an agreement with the homeland of world socialism?

The signs had, in fact, been there for Kremlin watchers for some time. In March, in a veiled reference in a speech to the Party Congress, Stalin had warned the western democracies that the USSR would not be prepared to pull other people's 'chestnuts out of the fire for them'. In May, he had replaced his pro-Western, pro-League of Nations Foreign Minister Litvinov with the sycophantic yes-man Molotov. By early August, Britain and France were now sufficiently exercised to send a mission to Moscow to try and get a Russian alliance. The dawdling progress of the British mission over a sea voyage lasting three weeks, was scarcely likely to create a good impression in Moscow even if one modern historian suggests (oddly) that it was motivated by a desire to avoid German-occupied territory.

The crucial issue, however, was the problem of transit rights for the Red Army across Poland and Rumania. Without these rights, the Soviet Union could do nothing to help the Poles if they were attacked. They were not granted because Poland and Rumania feared that if they once let the Russians in, they would never get them out again.

So the Anglo-French talks with Stalin stalled, and Hitler saw his chance. He, after all, could offer Stalin the two independent Baltic Republics of Latvia and Estonia, as well as Eastern Poland, without a qualm. In comparison, the West had nothing to offer except a war to save the Poles, whom the USSR had little reason to love anyway. The Nazi-Soviet pact, therefore, though a profound shock for Chamberlain and all his colleagues, was a logical result of Soviet and Nazi objectives.

For Hitler, of course, the Nazi-Soviet pact seemed to be the supreme triumph. He could now, he thought, proceed with his attack on Poland without fear of interference. Alternatively, he could force the Poles to hand over Danzig and the Corridor, and become a satellite state of Germany. Surely Britain and France, deprived of the Soviet alliance, dared not interefere?

This time, however, Hitler had gone one step too far. Chamberlain's response on 25 August was to make the alliance with Poland into a formal military treaty. France, too, said she would stand by the Poles. Hitler was sufficiently taken aback by this to postpone his plan to attack Poland on 26 August.

BRITAIN GOES TO WAR

Even at this late stage, Chamberlain hoped that Britain's determination to stand by Poland would cause Hitler to think again, even if such determination had not materialised into any real help for the Poles. By September 1939, Britain had sent them just 44 planes and 700 guns.

The Anglo-Polish alliance did not, however, deter Hitler any more than the Nazi-Soviet pact intimidated Britain and France into abandoning Poland. Hitler merely moved his invasion date back to 1 September and Chamberlain desperately continued to try and preserve the peace. So did the Pope, the Queen of the Netherlands and assorted amateur diplomats sent by Hitler's colleague, Hermann Goering. But Hitler was determined to have his war.

War duly came on 1 September when German troops invaded Poland and German aircraft bombed Polish cities. Chamberlain continued to hope against hope that war could be avoided, and he incurred a good deal of odium for postponing the declaration of war until 3 September. In reality this was largely a result of the Government's attempt to get Britain's declaration into line with France's, which still came six hours later. This so infuriated some of Chamberlain's Cabinet colleagues that they insisted that an ultimatum be sent to the Germans, requiring them to get out of Poland by 11 am on 3 September.

Chamberlain then made this broadcast to the British people:

> Everything I have worked for, everything that I have hoped for, everything that I have believed in during my public life, has crashed into ruins. There is only one thing left for me to do: that is, to devote what strength and powers I have to forwarding the victory of the cause for which we have to sacrifice so much. I cannot tell what part I shall be allowed to play myself . . .

Strangely, this statement, a sad and sombre one, has been criticised by some historians because of its emphasis on Chamberlain's personal feelings. But his feelings were genuine and patriotic. No one had laboured harder for peace than he had.

timeline		
	May 1937	Neville Chamberlain becomes Prime Minister
	March 1938	The Anschluss
	September 1938	The Munich Conference
	March 1939	Hitler annexes Czech lands. Slovakia becomes independent republic. British guarantee to Poland
	August 1939	Nazi-Soviet Pact
	September 1939	Britain declares war on Germany

Points to consider

1) Discuss the ways in which Chamberlain's view of foreign policy differed from that of Eden and Churchill.

2) 'A cruel necessity.' Do you agree with this judgement on the Munich Agreement?

3) Why, in March 1939, did Neville Chamberlain give Poland the guarantee he had refused to Czechoslovakia six months before?

4) What does Table 3 tell us about British defence policy in 1938?

5) What, if anything, was new about Chamberlain's foreign policy between March and September 1939?

6) 'Everything I have worked for . . . has crashed into ruins.' What had Neville Chamberlain been working for in his foreign policy and why had he failed?

7) 'Hitler's War.' Is this the only explanation for the outbreak of the Second World War in September 1939?

9

THE LAST PHASE

Neville Chamberlain viewed the prospect of war with no enthusiasm. Before its outbreak he believed 'no one else could carry out my policy', but afterwards he thought half a dozen people could have led the country. Thoughts of the First World War and its terrible burden of human suffering filled him with horror.

His hope was that there would be a social collapse inside Germany, brought on by economic weakness, which would avoid the need for the horrific slaughter of the earlier war. 'Time,' Chamberlain believed, 'is with us.' This view was not as absurd as it has sometimes been made out to be. Recent research by historians like Richard Overy has shown that ordinary German citizens had to undergo a great deal of privation in the winter of 1939-40. Rationing, for example, was far more rigorous in Germany during the first winter of the war than it was in Britain. For Hitler, war in 1939 was at least two years too soon and against the wrong enemies (the USSR being seen as Germany's arch enemy).

Chamberlain's hope that there would be a war of economic attrition, with the Allies blockading Germany with their superior navies, accorded with French policy as well. But the French wanted above all to keep the war off their own soil, and sponsored the rather bizarre idea of distant campaigns in the Balkans and the Caucasus (to stop the Germans getting oil from there). Nevertheless, even the French generals were confident of ultimate victory and Chamberlain, like Churchill, believed them. He can hardly be blamed for accepting such widespread assumptions in Britain that the great French army would perform as heroically as it had done in World War One.

Chamberlain has been blamed for the lackadaisacal conduct of the so-called 'phoney war' between October 1939 and April 1940, and there is some weight behind this criticism. For a government minister to prohibit the bonbing of arms dumps in the Black Forest (as one did) because it was 'private property' was plainly absurd. Nor were leaflet raids on Germany, tellings its citizens they could not win the war, likely to make Hitler surrender. What Chamberlain failed to realise was that Hitler did intend to attack in the West after the rapid collapse of the Poles in September 1939, and failed to do so immediately only because of bad weather during the winter of 1930-40.

CHAMBERLAIN AND CHURCHILL

The only active sector in the war was at sea, which fell under Churchill's auspices as First Lord of the Admiralty. He presided over the operation in December 1939 which resulted in the sinking of the German pocket battleship *Graf Spee* (strictly speaking, scuttling, as the German ship was sunk by its captain in Montevideo harbour). More than this, Churchill irritated Chamberlain by interfering in other areas of War Cabinet responsibility, and by his locquacity in Cabinet discussions.

Churchill was the advocate of a more positive extension of the war, a prospect frankly dreaded by the Prime Minister, and was a strong advocate of intervention on the side of Finland in her war with the USSR during the winter of 1939-40. This intervention, which would have involved Britain in a war with Germany and the USSR simultaneously, would have been a disaster reminiscent of the Gallipoli fiasco in the First World War, but fortunately for the British, Finnish resistance collapsed in March 1940.

CABINET MANAGEMENT

Relations with Churchill, who was never an easy colleague, did underline a rather negative aspect of Chamberlain's premiership. He complained about the low calibre of many of his Conservative colleagues, yet had excluded Churchill from his pre-war administration precisely because he was a powerful personality with ideas of his own (suggestions from Home Secretary Hoare that Churchill be brought into the Government early in 1939 were rejected out of hand by Chamberlain).

Chamberlain's Cabinets therefore had an aura of time-serving about them, although leading figures like Halifax and Hoare were wholehearted supporters of the appeasement policy. Ironically, one of the few more outspoken members of the Chamberlain Cabinet, Leslie Hoare-Belisha, was removed from his post as Secretary of State for War in January 1940 in circumstances which did Chamberlain little credit. Hoare-Belisha had made himself unpopular with the Commanders of the British Army in France by making some quite justified criticisms of its dispositions, and became the victim of a sinister anti-Semitic whispering campaign against him in establishment circles. Chamberlain did offer him another post, but his failure to stand by his Minister (Belisha turned down the offer and left the Government) showed the Prime Minister in a poor light. Chamberlain had never usually been a man who brooked interference in ministerial appointments.

The other major criticism that can be made of Chamberlain in the last phase of his prime ministership was that he was not fitted to be a wartime leader, and that he knew this to be the case. 'How I hate and loathe this war,' he wrote. 'I was never meant to be a War Minister.' Why then did he not resign, and allow Churchill, whom he recognised to be a natural war leader (and had taken into his government as first Lord of the Admiralty), to take over? The question is quite easily answered. In the first place, he felt it was his duty to soldier on, but more importantly, he knew that Churchill did not have the support of the Conservative Party which at that stage was not in a wartime coalition with the other parties. Chamberlain can be criticised for running the war as a Conservative war, but he was right about Churchill. Even when Churchill became Prime Minister in 1940, he remained unpopular with the bulk of the Tory Party and was aware of it.

CHAMBERLAIN'S FALL
—

In April 1940, Chamberlain made an unfortunate gaffe on the lines of his earlier notorious 'peace in our time' remark after Munich; 'Hitler' he said, has missed the bus'. Only days later, German forces invaded Denmark and Norway, partly as a response to Allied plans to interfere with German iron ore supplies from Sweden.

Britain and France could do nothing to save Denmark, but they did send an expeditionary force to Norway, which unfortunately arrived too late to prevent the Germans overrunning that country. Although primary responsibility for the Norway campaign fell to Winston Churchill who had to get the expeditionary force there, the odium for its failure fell on Neville Chamberlain. This was the background for the famous debate of 7-8 May 1940 which resulted in Neville Chamberlain's downfall.

Chamberlain appeared to be quite safe because he had a large Parliamentary majority, and he certainly saw no reason to resign because of the Norway fiasco. But he misjudged the mood of the House of Commons which now included a large number of Tories who were perturbed about the conduct of the war. Among several memorable interventions on the conduct of the Norway Campaign was one from Leo Amery, all the more damaging because it came from an ex-Cabinet colleague and fellow Birmingham MP of many years' standing. With devastating effect, Amery quoted Oliver Cromwell's comments to a seventeenth-century parliament and demanded of the Chamberlain government: 'You have sat here for too long for any good you have been doing. In the name of God go!'

Churchill remained loyal to the government, as he was bound to do as a Cabinet minister, but Chamberlain's arch enemy, Lloyd George, intervened to warn the First Lord of the Admiralty not to become an air raid shelter protecting the Government from the splinters of criticism thrown at it. An admiral of the fleet in full uniform with medals also intervened to castigate Chamberlain about Norway.

When the vote was taken, Chamberlain still had a majority of 81 votes. But 30 Conservatives had voted with he Opposition, and another 60 had abstained. Undoubtedly, some Tories had been angered by Chamberlain's reference, shaken as he was by the savage attack on him, to 'my friends' in the House who would support him. This was regarded as a partisan remark in what was supposed to be a national emergency.

The vote after the Norway debate did not, though, dispose Chamberlain to go. In fact, he was buoyed up by the news on 10 May that Hitler had attacked France, Belgium, Holland and Luxemburg. But he did deem it necessary to now form a coalition government with Labour and the Liberals.

Labour, after some hesitation, flatly refused to serve under Chamberlain. This factor was crucial in Chamberlain's eventual decision to resign, as was the advice from the Chancellor of the Exchequer, Sir Kingsley Wood, that he must resign if Labour refused to serve under him. Coming from such a quarter (Wood had been his Parliamentary Private Secretary from 1924-9 and remained a close adviser), this advice undoubtedly undermined

Chamberlain's morale on 10 May. The historians, Gilbert and Gott, remark that 'Neville Chamberlain expected more from an old friend. Such loyalty was denied him'. He therefore tendered his resignation to the King that very day.

Chamberlain's preferred successor was Lord Halifax, the former Viceroy in India and a man closely associated with the appeasement policy. He was undoubtedly the choice, too, of the bulk of the Tory party. Labour might well have served under Halifax, who was also the choice of George IV, but in an interview between Chamberlain, Churchill and the Foreign Secretary, Halifax, allegedly (according to Churchill's memoirs) said he could not be Prime Minister because he was in the House of Lords. Churchill therefore, became Prime Minister by default, with Labour support.

But Churchill did not secure the immediate loyalty of the Conservative party, and Chamberlain remained Conservative party leader. Churchill knew that he needed Chamberlain to secure the backing of the Conservatives, and so Chamberlain became Lord President of the Council in the new coalition government. In that capacity he served Churchill faithfully until the end of his life. He himself was to recognise the correctness of Churchill's appointment later, saying that 'In the more active phase of the war I feel that Winston is the right man for the head in view of his experience and study of war'. And, as John Charmley points out, Chamberlain's new role did him credit, for he 'unlike Asquith in the last war, stayed on to help the new Prime Minister'.

CHAMBERLAIN'S DEATH

After his fall from power, Neville Chamberlain's health declined rapidly. In February 1940, he had written to one of his sisters saying how his health had stood up better to the strain of office (he was over 70) than Joseph Chamberlain's had done. But after the events of 10 May, which had been a severe blow to a proud man, he noted how 'I had lost my spring and my spirits'. Cancer of the bowel was diagnosed, operations failed, and on 22 September, Chamberlain sent Churchill his letter of resignation.

Shortly afterwards, with the agreement of King Geoge VI, Churchill offered Chamberlain a knighthood but he declined the offer saying that he preferred to die 'like his father, plain Mr. Chamberlain'. Sadly, he wrote to Stanley Baldwin that 'I doubt if I shall ever visit Brum again'. In the event, he did not, for death came for Neville Chamberlain on 9 November, at Highfield House near the village of Heckfield.

A service of commemoration was held for him on November 14 in Westminster Abbey, and he was buried next to Andrew Bonar Law who had given him his first government posts nearly twenty years before. Two days earlier, Winston Churchill had told the House of Commons:

> Whatever else history may or may not say about these terrible tremendous years, we may be sure that Neville Chamberlain acted with perfect sincerity according to his lights and strove to the utmost of his capacity and authority, to save the world from the awful, devastating struggle in which we are now engaged. This alone will stand him in good stead as far as what is called the verdict of history is concerned.

RETROSPECT

It was long fashionable to blame Neville Chamberlain for the disasters that befell Britain and her allies in 1940. At least he, unlike Baldwin, was largely spared in death the abuse of whose who wanted a scapegoat to blame for the fact that Britain found herself, allegedly ill-prepared, at war. Some criticism was levied at Chamberlain in his last months, and he was pained by it.

Was it deserved? Chamberlain was not a man of war, was depressed by the prospect of it, and adopted a strategy designed to avoid bloodshed as long as possible. He may be thought naive in his hope that economic rather than military collapse might have brought Nazi Germany to its knees.

Yet Chamberlain's assessment was shared by many others, and was not, as it has been often claimed, defeatist. The French generals, for all their apparent inaction in 1939-40, were confident that Germany could and would be beaten. Neither, as has been claimed, was the Anglo-French alliance borne down upon by a torrent of Nazi tanks and planes in 1940. In actual fact the Allies had more aircraft and tanks than the Germans, but their tactics were wrong. Even Churchill, that keen student of war, was taken aback by the speed and ruthlessness of the German *Blitzkreig*. But the result was by no means a foregone conclusion, and modern military historians have emphasised how more resolute French leadership in 1940 could have produced a different result.

Is it, therefore, right to criticise Neville Chamberlain when the men of war and politicians who have lambasted his appeasement policy got it wrong? Was Britain ill prepared?

In one sense, yes. The British Expeditionary Force that was sent to France in 1939-40 was too small, inadequately equipped, and was not the significant contribution to the French war effort it should have been. But then no one expected the great French army to collapse in such a rapid manner as it did in 1939-40.

Chamberlain was, of course, responsible for the limited British commitment on land, but this is precisely *because* he (and Churchill) had such confidence in the French army. He is open to the accusation that for many years the army had been the Cinderella of the armed services. But so is Churchill, who in the 1920s presided over swingeing cuts in the armed services as Chancellor of the Exchequer.

Conversely, Chamberlain did accelerate the expansion of the RAF which allowed it to win the Battle of Britain in the summer of 1940. He died in the knowledge at least that the German invasion planned for that year had been beaten off, and beaten off by the modernised RAF with radar and Spitfires. But this expansion, too, was carried out against Chamberlain's own instinct for as his former colleague, Lord Swinton (Air Minister 1935-8) wrote:

> He was the most pacific and honourable of men: the vast expenditure of money on rearming was something which shocked him; his mind could not reconcile itself to the justification of a massive arms programme.

But reconcile himself he did, to the tune of £1500 million, as both Chancellor and Prime Minister, even if Swinton and others thought this was not enough.

Neville Chamberlain's career has aroused controversy among historians, and will continue to do so. In his recent sympathetic treatment of Chamberlain and his appeasement policy, Charmley concludes that:

> The 'Guilty Men' Syndrome [a reference to a notorious anti-Chamberlain pamphlet produced in 1940] has run its course, and Chamberlain's reputation stands better now than it has ever done . . . The venom of his opponents pursued him long, but his was the only policy which offered any hope of avoiding war – and of saving both lives and the British Empire.

Charmley overstates his case because Chamberlain's policy was not the 'only policy' available, and it is doubtful, too, whether the 'Guilty Men' syndrome has entirely run its course. Even in 1991, a biography of Lord Halifax could still throw up the old accusations about humourlessness, vanity and arrogance. Nevertheless, there is now, as was not the case in the past, a disposition to take into account the many variables and considerable dilemmas which Neville Chamberlain had to face during his premiership. We need not doubt the accuracy of the plaque erected to his memory in Heckfield village church:

'Write me as one that loves his fellow-men.'

WAS CHAMBERLAIN A FAILURE?

By his own lights Neville Chamberlain was a failure. He admitted as much in his broadcast on the outbreak of war in September 1939. The appeasement policy was, after all, designed to improve relations with Germany and avoid war, and it did neither. Anti-appeasers blamed Chamberlain, perhaps rightly, for failing to realise that Britain could never have harmonious relations with a German government under Hitler (a colleague of Ambassador Henderson in Berlin told him that his mission could not be regarded as a failure because no one could have succeeded in Nazi Germany). Chamberlain would doubtless have retorted that the effort to preserve the peace was supremely worth making, but did his anxiety to do so cause him to lose his sense of what was possible? Politics, is after all, as Chamberlain's colleague, R.A. Butler (Under Secretary at the Foreign Office) wrote many years later, 'the art of the possible'. In assessing Chamberlain's overall record, however, it is surely just to balance the foreign policy failure against his considerable domestic achievement, particularly in the 1920s.

timeline	September 1939	Outbreak of War
	April 1940	Denmark and Norway invaded by Germans
	May 1940	Hitler attacks France and the Low Countries
		Fall of the Chamberlain Government
	November 1940	Death of Neville Chamberlain

Issues to consider

1) **Outline Chamberlain's strategy in 1939-40.**
2) **Explain the circumstances of Chamberlain's fall in May 1940, and account for his continued service in the government.**

BIBLIOGRAPHY

Aster, Sidney, 'Guilty Men', in Boyce and Robertson (eds) *Paths to War*, Macmillan London, 1989.

Bell, P.M.H., *The Origins of the Second World War*, Longman, London, 1988. Very clearly written and accessible to most A level students.

Charmley, John, *Chamberlain and the Lost Peace*, Hodder & Stoughton, London, 1989. Too detailed for most, but a useful antidote to the 'Umbrella Man' school of historians.

Dilks, David, *Neville Chamberlain, Vol. 1, 1869–1929*, Cambridge University Press, Cambridge, 1984. The definitive biography but too complex for the mainstream A level student without teacher direction.

Jenkins, Roy, *Baldwin*, London, 1990. Readable and interesting about Chamberlain as well as Baldwin.

Kennedy, Paul, The Rise and Fall of the Great Powers, *Unwin Hyman, London, 1988*. Probably more suitable for undergraduates than A level students without explicit guidance.

Lamb, Richard, *The Drift to War, 1922–39*, Bloomsbury, London, 1989. A traditional 'Chamberlain Basher'. A useful antidote to Charmley.

Middlemass, K. and Barnes, J., *Baldwin*, Widenfeld and Nicolson, London, 1969. Detailed and definitive, to be consulted with teacher direction.

Montgomery-Hyde, H., *Neville Chamberlain*, in A.J.P. Taylor (ed.), British Prime Minsters series, Widenfeld and Nicolson, London, 19xx. A short and readable study suitable for A level.

Rock, William R., *British Appeasement in the 1930s*, Edward Arnold, London, 1977. Short and accessible. Suitable for more able A level students.

Taylor, A.J.P., *English History 1914–45*, Oxford University Press, Oxford, 1965. Stimulating and within the capabilities of the majority of A level students.

Taylor, A.J.P., *The Origins of the Second World War*, Hamish Hamilton, London, 1961. Highly controversial analysis. Probably too detailed for A level, but an awareness of its main thesis is essential.

The following articles from the *Modern History Review* are particularly well tailored to the needs of the A level student.

Stuart Ball, 'The Conservative Dominance', Nov 1991.

Richard Cockett, 'Britain's Prime Minister in the Dock', Feb 1990.

Peter Catterel, 'The Opposition Attitude to War; Labour and Appeasement', Feb 1990.

Peter Neville, 'Neville Chamberlain, the Maligned Prime Minister', Sept 1992.

Philip Taylor, 'Appeasement. Guilty Men or Guilty Conscience?', Nov 1989.

In addition, the following film is available from the British Universities Film and Video Council: *Neville Chamberlain* (1975), B&W, 27 minutes. Archive serial number 1. It is a compilation of eight newsreel stories from the 1930s, with notes available.

INDEX